The Resilient Leader

How to beat being overwhelmed and burnout for sustainable leadership

Dr AMANDA NICKSON

First published by Ultimate World Publishing 2022
Copyright © 2022 Amanda Nickson

ISBN

Paperback: 978-1-922714-93-0
Ebook: 978-1-922714-94-7

Amanda Nickson has asserted her rights under the Copyright, Designs and Patents Act 1988 to be identified as the author of this work. The information in this book is based on the author's experiences and opinions. The publisher specifically disclaims responsibility for any adverse consequences which may result from use of the information contained herein. Permission to use information has been sought by the author. Any breaches will be rectified in further editions of the book.

All rights reserved. No part of this publication may be reproduced, stored in or introduced into a retrieval system, or transmitted in any form, or by any means (electronic, mechanical, photocopying, recording or otherwise) without the prior written permission of the author. Any person who does any unauthorised act in relation to this publication may be liable to criminal prosecution and civil claims for damages. Enquiries should be made through the publisher.

Cover design: Ultimate World Publishing
Layout and typesetting: Ultimate World Publishing
Editor: Isabelle Russell
Cover photo: Rachael Bourke, Be Still Bourke Photography

Ultimate World Publishing
Diamond Creek,
Victoria Australia 3089
www.writeabook.com.au

Testimonials

We live in a frenetic world, with constant demands on our time and energy, and it becomes difficult to get off the spinning wheel of achievement. Amanda's book makes clear that we must self-care. Each chapter is honest and vulnerable, practical and insightful. Amanda provides grounded accessible steps to avoid and/or recover from burnout. And for those who need more, there are more recommendations at the end of each chapter. A must-read for all high achievers!
Penny Mulvey, Chief Wellbeing and Communications Officer, Bible Society Australia

Amanda's passion to equip others to live life to the fullest is evident through her books, her conversations and her own remarkable resilience. I met Amanda through our joint interest in supervision, both passionate about walking alongside others, empowering people to connect to their calling, to live authentically and to have confidential, non-judgemental support. I would describe Amanda as someone who has a solid faith and on whom you can really rely. It's out of this steadfastness, along with her vast experience and qualifications, that she can share with others how to build resilience.

Susan Marcuccio, National Supervision Director, Chaplaincy Australia and Supervisor, Perspective Supervision

When it comes to leadership, resilience is the emotional, cognitive and behavioural capacity and capability to adapt and thrive in adverse environments and respond swiftly and appropriately to these changes and challenges. How do we develop sustainable resilience? What does compassion satisfaction have to do with resilience? These are some of the questions that Dr Amanda Nickson addresses in her brilliant book, The Resilient Leader. *I have known Amanda for almost 30 years and have observed this kind of resilience throughout her life. Her experiences, knowledge and learning are the basis for this book and will inspire and inform you. A must-read book for every leader.*

Cami De Almeida, Leadership Coach and Facilitator, Founder ViGEO Life and Leadership Development

It is my joy to commend Amanda Nickson to you. She has a passion for helping and supporting ministers and Church leaders and has the necessary skills to provide some very insightful comments. Church leaders are under increasing pressure these days from many directions, and resignation rates are very high. Amanda deals daily with hurting people and is very keen to provide support and help to those in Christian leadership. I recommend reading this book.

Rev Anne Harley, Combined Churches Townsville

Sometimes it happens – you meet somebody at the right time in your life, for the right reasons and know that your paths will cross for decades to come. That is how it is with Amanda. She is knowledgeable, gentle and a wise person who is authentic in her faith and is well experienced and qualified to help pastors, chaplains and Christian leaders understand resilience to last the distance while they serve others.

Amanda equips others with resilience skills and, most importantly, she lives it! Over the years, Amanda has continued to inspire me with her work, her contribution to those around her, living by faith on a day-to-day basis and her genuine desire to support those in leadership with self-care strategies so they can avoid emotional exhaustion. Dr Amanda Nickson has a unique combination of professional expertise, lived experience of resilience and a calling to support others to prevent burnout which enables her to instil confidence in all those she engages with whether that be in a personal or professional setting.
    Dr Rhonda Emonson, Mediator, Resilience Coach, Counsellor. Albury, NSW Australia

Amanda is living proof of resilience and tenacity. She has experienced burnout and understands the importance of self-care, kindness and self-compassion. She carries herself gently and generously shares her firsthand experiences.
    Jennifer Blackshaw, Director Organisational Services, Townsville Catholic Education

Disclaimer

All examples are based on real life situations. Some stories and details have been combined and changed to protect the identities of the people involved.

Dedication

To Jess, Danielle and Tim,
you continue to inspire me to do more.

Thank you for who you are and your love for me.

Contents

Testimonials	iii
Dedication	ix
Introduction	xiii
Chapter 1: Win the Burnout Battle	1
Chapter 2: From Compassion Fatigue to Compassion Satisfaction	15
Chapter 3: The Roadmap to Build Resilience	23
Chapter 4: The Power of Professional Supervision	33
Chapter 5: Physical Sustainability	41
Chapter 6: Emotional Sustainability	51
Chapter 7: Psychological Sustainability	59
Chapter 8: Social Sustainability	67
Chapter 9: Spiritual Sustainability	75
Chapter 10: Empowering Emerging Leaders	83
Chapter 11: The Encouragement Ethos	91
Chapter 12: Walk the Path for Others to Follow	99
Appendices	105
Afterword	109
About the Author	111
Other Books by the Author	113
Acknowledgements	115
Speaker Bio	117
Offers and Call to Action	119

Introduction

The Resilient Leader: How to beat being overwhelmed and burnout for sustainable leadership, has been on my heart to write for some time, as I've reflected on the number of times I've witnessed church pastors, leaders and social workers leaving their positions due to burnout, or being close to it. This book outlines some of the key causes of burnout and looks at several self-care strategies. I have been a leader in local churches and as a social worker for over 37 years and have sadly seen many good leaders and workers leave for numerous reasons which will be discussed in these pages.

In writing this book, I have reflected on my own experiences as a pastor's wife to my husband, Daryl, in Central Queensland, leading two churches in the mining towns of Middlemount and Dysart for four years in the eighties. Back then, the role of a pastor's wife was not well defined. I was working full-time as a social worker for the first two years while my husband served as pastor, as well as working another full-time job. We were the ministry team for the two churches. We lived in Middlemount and held a service on Sunday morning there, then on Sunday nights we drove to Dysart, another mining town about an hour's drive away.

After the birth of our first child, I left my social work role and had a part-time stint as a photojournalist for the local newspaper. I was able to lead a weekly women's Bible study in Dysart and would drive up for one day each week with my daughter while Daryl was at work managing a caravan park. I also did some contract social work jobs for the mining company there and for the Department of Child Safety. Both churches were very small with a group of faithful families attending in each location. I played the keyboard and led the music every week for both services. We held some creative community activities including a go-kart race, and I directed a musical involving most of the church members and much of the Middlemount community. Both Daryl and I greatly enjoyed our time there.

After four years, however, we felt we'd come to the end of everything we knew to do. We'd run out of ideas, as well as steam. We were exhausted and felt that we weren't getting anywhere. The churches were both small and had not experienced much growth. This was in the era when numbers were a real talking point at pastors' meetings and conferences. We decided to move to Townsville to be closer to Daryl's parents for a while so that they could see their granddaughter. For context, we were working as a pastor and pastor's wife in a mining town, where most of the people in the town were on very high incomes, where nearly every family was affected by shift work and education was not particularly valued by the majority of people, which was very challenging.

When we arrived in Townsville, we were encouraged to serve and to be leaders in our local church, still in ministry, just not "the pastor". My husband has since moved through numerous jobs, never returning to the role of a pastor. He has served in the children's ministry, youth ministry, leading small home groups and is now passionate about doing business to support the church. We have

Introduction

both served for years in numerous leadership capacities. I have been on church boards serving as a secretary and treasurer. I've been responsible for church welfare or care programs, I have been on music teams, led home groups, connect groups, prayer meetings and served on service teams. I've cleaned toilets and bathrooms, kitchens and floors, and I've preached. I have come to fulfill later in life the call on my life I've always had to be in ministry as a pastor. In 2021, I became a pastor of the Australian Christian Churches (ACC).

A few years ago, for the fourth time, I was also very close to burnout in my professional social work role in a busy job with a high workload and the added pressure of juggling part-time study, three children and church responsibilities. This experience is not unique. In fact, it is all too common.

This book is helpful for anyone wanting to look at ways to avoid and overcome burnout through the following chapters:

1. Chapter 1 – Winning the burnout battle and prevention is the best cure
2. Chapter 2 – Compassion fatigue and how to increase compassion satisfaction
3. Chapter 3 – How to build resilience and the many factors that this involves
4. Chapter 4 – The role of professional supervision and how valuable this can be
5. Chapter 5 – Emotional sustainability
6. Chapter 6 – Physical sustainability and what we can do to work on our health and wellbeing
7. Chapter 7 – Psychological and academic sustainability to be leaders long-term
8. Chapter 8 – The importance of social connections as we are not meant to do life alone

9. Chapter 9 – Spiritual sustainability and the many ways we can build our spiritual strength
10. Chapter 10 – Empowering emerging leaders and what we can do to safeguard against burn-out and other traps
11. Chapter 11 – The importance of encouragement
12. Chapter 12 – Next steps to influence policy and practice for leaders

Throughout this book, I hope you find keys and tools that equip you to live your journey as a leader for the long term.

Chapter 1

Win the Burnout Battle

The road to burnout is easy when you care for others. There is always more that you can do – more needs to respond to, more expectations from those in positions above us, more expectations from the people you serve, and more expectations for ourselves all add extra pressure.

So, why do we need to talk about burnout? Burnout can be devastating. Some people never fully recover or return to their calling. Prevention is the best cure and better than dealing with recovery. The risk is real. The needs and opportunities around us can be overwhelming. We need to be able to stay long-term in the vocation we have chosen. Some ministers burn out, leave ministry and never return. Some even leave the faith altogether. Brian Dodd, author and leadership coach (https://briandoddonleadership.com/) has stated that, "The pastoral profession has one of the top three suicide rates of any profession" (pastors coming third after doctors and lawyers).

What is burnout? The Merriam-Webster dictionary defines burnout as "exhaustion of physical or emotional strength or motivation, usually as a result of prolonged stress or frustration."

Stress is a state of mental tension and worry caused by problems in your life or work. Cumulative stress increases with each additional stressor.

We all go through stressful events in life. If there is some time for recovery, we get back to our equilibrium or balance. But what happens when there are several stressful events close together, one after another? The body and mind do not have a chance to recover – we are still in an elevated state of stress. Our "at rest" stress level is still up. This can continue until our stress levels are so high, even the smallest final straw can break the camel's back.

When our physical and emotional strength is totally spent and we feel we are unable to go on, this could be burnout. There are many indicators for burnout that are usually uncharacteristic of your usual behaviour, such as:

- Not wanting to see another person or hear another request
- Having no concern for the welfare of someone else
- Exhaustion or fatigue
- Irritability
- Negativity
- Feelings of inadequacy
- Reduced empathy
- Feeling isolated
- A sense of overwhelm or despair
- Conflicts in relationships
- Withdrawal and reduced intimacy
- Insomnia

- Purposelessness or a reduced sense of making a difference or satisfaction
- Reduced effectiveness and productivity
- Tension headaches
- Upset stomach
- High blood pressure
- Anxiety and depression

It is interesting that in the Bible, Elijah seems to experience burnout in 1 Kings 19. After Elijah's great victory against the 450 prophets of Baal in 1 Kings 18, a person threatens to kill him, and Elijah runs away and hides alone in the wilderness. He appears to be exhausted and pleads with God to end his life! God allows him to sleep and provides food and water for him. God listens to Elijah's worries and concerns. Elijah is reminded of God's power in the storms and provision and is soon restored to go on to a new task. Elijah rested, sought and listened to God and was then refreshed to resume serving.

An example of burnout in my own life happened a few years ago when I was attending a small church that was reaching out to numerous newly arrived African refugees living in Townsville. Many were Christians wanting to attend a local church. It was an opportunity to serve people who really needed some help. My husband really enjoyed the church and was able to communicate well with and help some of the men in the congregation in all sorts of ways. I was trying to connect with the women who had very limited English. Many of the male refugees had much better English than their wives. There were also some women who were heading households on their own, often having come from very traumatic situations. Another problem for this group was that many families didn't have transport and there was no public transport. The private bus company in town had very limited services on a

Sunday and some routes did not operate on Sunday at all. It was difficult for these families to access the church that was meeting in a building at a university. Some families had several children, so it was difficult to even pick up a family in an average vehicle. I asked the pastor if it would be helpful for me to borrow a minibus to see if we could help transport some of these families who didn't have their own transport.

He was agreeable to the idea. I therefore approached one of the local high schools where my own children attended school and was able to negotiate a contract with the school to borrow their minibus every Sunday morning. I went back to the pastor with this news, excited, and asked him, "So, who do you want to do the pickup and to collect all the families on Sunday mornings?" He asked me to do it. I thought, "Oh, that wasn't what I had in mind." But it's hard to say no to a pastor when you're asked to do something. So, because I knew the need for transport, I agreed to be the person picking up the families. What this meant was every Sunday, I had to go to the school early, unlock the gate and then the shed where the bus was, take the bus out, lock up the school gates, do the rounds and pick up several families and their children and bring them to church, which I loved to do. It also meant that after I dropped everyone home, I had to clean the bus before locking up the shed and locking up the school gate before driving home. All up, being involved in these activities plus church on Sunday morning was about a six-hour commitment each Sunday from 7:30 am to about 1:30 pm.

I had to collect the keys for the school gate, shed and bus from the school each Friday before 4:00 pm when the school office closed and return them on Monday morning before 9:00 am. I had some other responsibilities in the church service as well. I was one of only two musicians and played the keyboard and often led the singing every week. I was on a roster to lead and teach the children a lesson during church once every couple of months as all the parents took a turn to lead the children's activities. This was an expectation. Again, as I had specifically been asked to do this, I did not feel I could say no. The church usually had a morning tea after church and during this time I was trying to speak with some of the refugee women, trying to build relationships, but anything more than a simple, "Hello, how are you?" was too much for the women to understand. The church service was being interpreted into Swahili so that these new families could understand the message. This meant the service took a long time, longer than I was used to. If I asked something like, "How is your son? He was sick last week," the woman would say, "I'll get my husband to translate," because they had very limited English. This limited the ability to connect with the women. I felt I couldn't really connect or have close personal conversations with any of the women in the church. It was too difficult to manage translation with an interpreter, husband or friend as part of this conversation. I was feeling isolated.

At the same time, I was also dealing with a very demanding full-time job as an academic; studying a PhD part-time and managing three children while my husband worked mainly night shifts. I was feeling more and more overwhelmed and exhausted emotionally, physically, spiritually – in every way. So, at the end of that year, after several months of doing the bus run, the music, trying to be a friend with the women, I simply stopped going to church. I just couldn't do it anymore. I was exhausted in every sense of the word, in contrast to my normal self. I was really shocked that this was where I was, but that's where I was.

After a few weeks staying home on Sunday mornings, my husband was still going to this same church, but he wasn't unhappy with my decision. He could understand it. I thought of a church I'd previously gone to where there were several other professional women that I knew and I thought, oh, I could go back to that church and just reconnect with some women there and get some support, nurturing, and encouragement – spiritually and emotionally. I needed connection as I felt so isolated. I needed re-filling, as I felt that I had given everything out and my own tank had run dry. I returned to the church I had attended for many years before and was welcomed back. I was able to immediately connect with a few people I'd known previously – it felt like I had come home.

After a few months of being ministered to and fellowshipping with other like-minded people, I was regaining my balance and strength and began to serve again.

So, how do we win the burnout battle?

Three ways to overcome and avoid burnout

1. Identify and manage your stress responses

Having an awareness of your own physical and emotional responses to stress by recognising and acting on them early, rather than ignoring them, is vital if you want to beat potential burnout. Do you recognise your own indicators of stress? It could be a tension headache, tense muscles in your neck and shoulders, an upset stomach or difficulty sleeping. These are the physical reactions. It could be affecting your ability to concentrate, or making decisions becomes harder. It is helpful to know the indicators. These can be different for each person. The human body has built-in early warning systems – it is wise not to ignore the warnings!

Once you have recognised that a reaction could be due to stress, it is important to put some time into de-stressing and relaxing. This is often easier said than done. Do you take stock of what is happening in your life when you experience such symptoms? Or do you ignore the headaches and press on regardless? Ignoring the early warning signs of chronic stress in your body can lead to significant health risks, including high blood pressure, a stroke or a heart attack.

More ideas on how to de-stress are in the "Additional information and resources" section at the end of the chapter.

2. The importance of setting boundaries
Saying no to some things so that you have the time to do the other things you have said yes to and to do them well.

I had been on a couple of committees in my workplace for over five years and I decided it was time to give them up in order to free up time to attend to other priorities. Each committee required several hours of preparation (for example, reading documents thoroughly) and work that needed to be done prior to attending the meetings. This was keeping me from doing other things that were a higher priority. I let it be known that I was no longer available for these committees. Even though I had built good working relationships within those committees, and we were making progress, I felt it was time to hand it over to someone else and claim back some time for myself. People tried to convince me to continue, to stay on for another year. I stood firm and said no to each committee. The arguments of, "It's not that much, you can do it," were given, but I stood my ground and continued with a firm no. I needed to make time for myself and more time for other roles and responsibilities I had in this job. As someone who has often been a people pleaser, not wanting to disappoint others, this was a major step for me.

Having clear boundaries can inform your priorities. Choosing your priorities – what is important for you, rather than feeling pressured to respond to the tyranny of the urgent (usually other people's priorities) – can be helpful. For example, if you have made plans in your diary for what you think is important to do that day and you find yourself being interrupted by other people's urgent agendas, you need to decide if this is really what you need to be doing right now. Being conscious of this is the first step in taking control of our time – a limited and precious resource.

More resources on boundaries can be found in the "Additional information and resources" section at the end of this chapter.

3. Making tough decisions

Sometimes we need to take stock and make a decision about, "Am I actually in the right place, in the right role, in the right job for me, at this time?" You may also need to decide to prioritise yourself – your own health and wellbeing. No one else can decide this for you.

After a period of time in a job where I was exhausted, continually stressed, overwhelmed and had a huge workload, I had a period of time off and I realised that I didn't want to go back. This role, which numerous other people thought was perfect for me, met all their requirements, ticked all the boxes and they thought was great for me, was not a good fit for me anymore. My priorities had changed, and I believed God was calling me to do other things. So, I made the tough decision of resigning from a permanent full-time position and took some time out for myself by running my own business part-time and contract work. This meant a huge reduction in income. I had been the main breadwinner for my family for several years, but I knew that prioritising my mental health was important. If I didn't change something, it was not going to be sustainable for me. It was not a decision I rushed into, and I had talked with my husband about it. He asked me to stay in the position for another year, and then another six months after that, so that we were not going to be financially stressed. This meant that, for 18 months, I continued in the job, all the while planning to leave. Even having an end date in mind was helpful to my wellbeing – I had a timeframe and I was working to it.

When I did leave, I felt so relieved. It was unbelievable. I was able to finally take a long holiday – for six weeks. For years, I would usually only take one or two weeks of holidays at a time adding up to the five weeks of annual leave I had each year. These were staggered across school holidays during the year to juggle looking after my children in the school holidays. The feeling of relief and replenishment that I was able to have knowing I wasn't coming back to a job that was causing me so much stress was brilliant. I was able to plan and participate in a fantastic walking and spiritual experience, the Camino Way, a walking trek and spiritual pilgrimage across Spain. This gave me an opportunity to reflect and get a different perspective on my life and to consider what I was going to do differently in the future. This time of reflection included how I was going to seek more balance with any work and the rest of my life. Having this time in nature, with more time to pray and time to reflect was so replenishing for me. It was good for my soul. I felt restored. I had deliberately chosen to spend time in nature, surrounded by natural beauty, which replenished me.

This was in fact renewing my mind, just as described in Romans 12:2: "Do not conform to the pattern of this world, but be transformed by the renewing of your mind."

Walking the Camino Way in Spain, 2018

Rev Mal York, St Andrews Anglican Church in Roseville, Sydney, has had some experiences with burnout that he has shared with me to help others through this book. He has been in ministry for 23 years and is a Chaplain for the New South Wales ambulance service. Rev York identified that there have been three times over his years in ministry where he had been in very challenging circumstances. One occurred about 10 years ago when his wife had cancer. He had several wonderful friends who provided extra support to him, his wife and children at that time that made a big difference in getting him through this challenging time. He has experienced situations where juggling a large congregation, a staff group and COVID stretched him in his ministry. These were exhausting and challenging times, and therefore he found it important to have strategies in place to find balance. Rev York identified three things that were particularly helpful when navigating tough times and challenging seasons:

Win the Burnout Battle

Still waters restoring my soul at Waterview Creek, Jourama Falls Camping area, Paluma Range National Park, 2021

1. Prayer with someone else. There is power and support in praying with another believer.
2. Having a support person, such as a mentor, who is available to provide support for you on your personal life journey. Rev York also attends a retreat and a renewal group regularly.
3. Engaging in regular physical exercise made a difference.

There is wisdom in these suggestions by Rev Mal York.

What ifs (objections and responses)

What if you decide to take some action and try to win this battle against burnout?

Objection 1: Saying no can seem selfish
Response: If you are *not* spread too thin and *can* act on and work on your priorities, you will do well and be more effective in getting done what you need to get done.

Objection 2: I can't prioritise or decide
Response: That sounds like you are stressed or overwhelmed. If you can get away to get some perspective and time out for reflection and then prioritise what is important that could make a difference.

Objection 3: Putting myself first seems wrong
Response: No, it's not. Unless you look after yourself, you are no good to anyone. You need to prioritise looking after yourself – no one else can do this for you.

Three actions to take

1. Consider and make some decisions about what is really important – your priorities.

2. Say no to some things that you have been asked to do. For example, do you have to be on that committee? Do you have to volunteer at that event?

3. Imagine what your de-stressed life would look like. How can you make it happen? For example, time for more meals with your family, time to exercise, time for more sleep. If you already feel burnt out, how can you regain your balance?

Remember

Matthew 11:28–30: "Come to me, all you who are weary and burdened, and I will give you rest. Take my yoke upon you and learn from me, for I am gentle and humble in heart, and you will find rest for your souls. For my yoke is easy and my burden is light."

Additional resources and information

Dr Henry Cloud and Dr John Townsend, *Boundaries* Grand Rapids, Michigan Zondervan 2013.

Brian Dodd https://briandoddonleadership.com/

Justine Toh *Achievement Addiction* https://www.reconsidering.com.au/

https://theresilienceproject.com.au/

NCLS Fact Sheet – Thriving and burnout
http://www.ncls.org.au/research/ncls-fact-sheet-14001

Health Promotion Centre, North Parramatta, *Learn to unwind: For health energy performance wellbeing* (1998).

Michael Tunnecliffe (1998) *How to Understand and manage stress* Bayside Books.

Francis, L. J., Robbins, M., & Wulff, K. (2013). Assessing the effectiveness of support strategies in reducing professional burnout among clergy serving in the Presbyterian Church (USA). *Practical Theology*, 6(3), 319–331.

Lewis, C. A., Turton, D. W., & Francis, L. J. (2007). Clergy work-related psychological health, stress, and burnout: An introduction to this special issue of Mental Health, Religion and Culture. *Mental Health, Religion & Culture*, 10(1), 1–8.

Miner, M. H., Dowson, M., & Sterland, S. (2010). Ministry orientation and ministry outcomes: Evaluation of a new multidimensional model of clergy burnout and job satisfaction. *Journal of Occupational and Organizational Psychology, 83*(1), 167–188.

Miner, M., Sterland, S., & Dowson, M. (2009). Orientation to the demands of ministry: Construct validity and relationship with burnout. *Review of religious research*, 463-479.

Parker, P. D., & Martin, A. J. (2011). Clergy motivation and occupational well-being: Exploring a quadripolar model and its role in predicting burnout and engagement. *Journal of Religion and Health, 50*(3), 656–674.

Randall, K. J. (2013). Clergy burnout: Two different measures. *Pastoral Psychology, 62*(3), 333-341.

Robbins, M., Francis, L., & Powell, R. (2012). Work-related psychological health among clergywomen in Australia. *Mental Health, Religion & Culture, 15*(9), 933-944.

https://www.businessthink.unsw.edu.au/articles/lucinda-brogden-leaders-workplace-mental-health

A copy of this chapter is available as a pdf for free from my website: https://www.amandanickson.com.au/ if you would like to pass this information on to others who may be interested.

More offers can be found at the end of the book.

Chapter 2

From Compassion Fatigue to Compassion Satisfaction

Without some compassion satisfaction, it can be very difficult to remain in a leadership role long-term.

Compassion is the sympathetic pity and concern for the sufferings or misfortunes of others (New Webster Dictionary).

Compassion fatigue is the emotional and physical fatigue from the chronic use of empathy, responding to people who are suffering in some way.

Compassion satisfaction, on the other hand, is a sense of appreciation; of being valued and understood and making a positive difference.

Compassion satisfaction leads to great job satisfaction and boosts our motivation. In contrast, compassion fatigue zaps our energy and motivation. We need to see results – the fruit of our labour – to be encouraged and satisfied that our efforts are having results and worth our while.

Hebrews Chapter 10: 24–25 says: "And let us consider how we may spur one another on toward love and good deeds, not giving up meeting together as some are in the habit of doing but encouraging one another and all the more as you see the day approaching." Being encouraged is so important in our work. Colossians 3:23 says, "Whatever you do, work at it with all your heart as working for the Lord, not for human masters."

Self-compassion is having understanding and being warm and loving to ourselves, especially when we feel inadequate, fail or suffer. It is showing kindness to ourselves – responding as we would if it were someone else who presented with these feelings or situations. Using self-compassion to look after ourselves enables us to look after others.

So, how does this all play out? Nickson, Carter and Francis (2020) write about compassion satisfaction and compassion fatigue, having identified both protective factors and risk factors for each. A table of these factors is at the end of the book in Appendix 1 at tables 1 and 2.

Some examples of protective factors against compassion fatigue include having a sense of meaning in your work, a safe and respectful workplace, continuing education, a reasonable workload, enjoying your work, peer support, sufficient sleep, regular physical exercise and having a balanced and nutritious diet. Risk factors could include excessive workloads, little or no supervision, insomnia, concentration difficulties, decision-making difficulties, loss of energy, purpose and meaning, emotional, spiritual and physical exhaustion, professional isolation and burnout.

Let's look an example of compassion fatigue in my own life. Drawing on the same situation as I described in Chapter 1 with the church which was predominantly made up of newly arrived refugee families, perhaps also because of my social work background, I knew many of the traumatic situations these families had come from. A young man who was 19 years of age was responsible for raising his five younger siblings as both his parents had been killed in unspeakable ways as the family had fled from a war zone. Then there was the single mother raising her four children on her own who had not only lost her husband, but had also been subjected to rape and torture by those taking power in her home country. The circumstances of each person and family group could be overwhelming, particularly if trying to respond and help using my own strength.

Even just looking at the congregation, I was experiencing emotional fatigue and compassion fatigue. I had been totally overwhelmed by the needs of so many of the people in this particular congregation – all I could see were needs and no way of meeting them all and at the same time feeling responsibility towards them. Women were wanting friendship and support and they needed help with English, negotiating systems such as the health system, schools, transport – so many different areas. Many had post-traumatic stress disorder (PTSD). My ultimate decision was to stop going to this church as I felt I could not do anymore as I was overwhelmed by the accumulation of their stories and circumstances and other stressors in my own life at that time.

A few months later in the church I returned to, I had become connected with lots of women. We all supported and were there for each other. I was asked to run a home group, a small group for women. I had so much satisfaction, compassion satisfaction doing this. I have a heart for single women, women who might be single parents or older mature women who are single. I felt I was able to make a difference and value them and see growth in their spiritual journey because we were able to connect on a regular basis. This was with a weekly group, and I also held a weekly prayer meeting. With both, I had a great sense that I was making a positive difference in their lives in small ways. And that gave me a great sense of compassion satisfaction. I was in a totally different place spiritually, emotionally and in every sense.

Another situation that illustrates compassion fatigue occurred several years ago when I worked as a senior social worker at Centrelink. The daily role included responding to "walk-ins" in crisis which could include people who were homeless, people fleeing situations of domestic violence and other situations of immediate need. As a large government department, it was often seen as the last port of call or last hope for help. I remember a situation where I was trying to assist a family who were homeless, living in a suburban park as it had a BBQ, a shelter shed and a toilet block. There was no emergency housing that could be found for a whole family immediately, as it was not a situation of domestic violence – this family group was both parents and their two children. They also wanted some assistance with being provided food. All the usual entitlements for finance had been already used and the best I could do was find a non-government agency that could provide a food hamper and deliver it to them in the park. They were very grateful. I was, however, gutted. I thought, "Wow, is this all our society can do for a family in crisis – drop off a food hamper to a park?" It made me really question the role I was in, society and the systems available to help people in crisis. I could see all the gaps and felt somewhat overwhelmed by the seeming impossibilities and challenges people faced trying to live day to day. I was feeling personally responsible even though I knew it was not up to me alone to solve all these gaps in the welfare services. I was exhausted and felt inadequate in my role because I had been unable to do more.

The cumulative effect of dealing with situation after situation such as this, unable to provide the desired outcome, contributed to emotional exhaustion and compassion fatigue. After I had been in that job for six years, I was able to take some long service leave and during my time off decided I really did not want to go back. I was done with responding to innumerable crisis situations daily. I did not feel I could face another crisis situation that I was unable to adequately find solutions to. It was during this time off that I decided to enrol in a PhD program, and I was miraculously offered a job at James Cook University soon afterwards, which I accepted.

I have also had times when I've needed to show myself self-compassion and to fill my own tank to be able to give out again. I have achieved this by going on walks to beautiful national parks or other places of beauty, such as looking at a beach or a sunrise or sunset, because that helps give me the ability to regain that balance. That is a way I have found that works for me to replenish my sense of wellbeing. I am a person who needs some time alone to recharge my batteries. Each of us has different things that help replenish our tanks. It is important that this is done in healthy ways. It's important to find what works for you.

Self-compassion includes being kind to ourselves rather than engaging in self-judgement. How do you choose to be kind to yourself? Maybe it means you take time out to have a cup of coffee or lunch with your friend or colleague rather than keeping going with the list of tasks for today.

Water tank, Hughenden

From Compassion Fatigue to Compassion Satisfaction

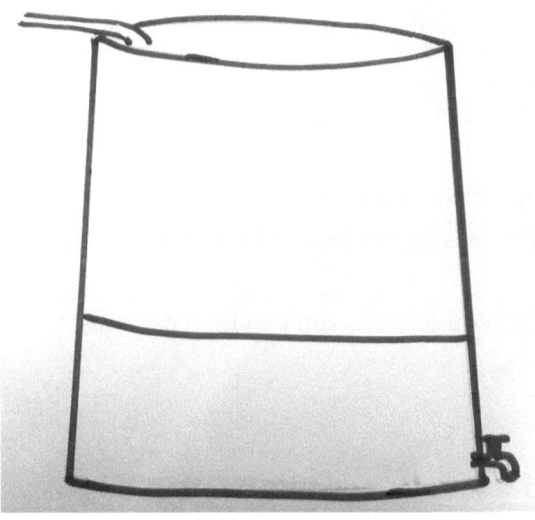

Diagram of our tank

What ifs

Objection 1: Isn't it selfish to look for compassion satisfaction?
Response: No, it's a part of your passion and part who you are. It fuels you to do more.

Objection 2: I shouldn't be avoiding showing compassion.
Response: Yes, sometimes you need to avoid situations that you know will cause you fatigue. You need to be in the role long-term. You need to know your boundaries. You may be able to help someone in some areas, but not in others. Know clearly when to delegate or to refer a person or situation on to someone else.

Objection 3: Showing self-compassion – isn't that self-centred?
Response: It may be, but it is to look after you for the long term. It's to build our sustainability. Remember Proverbs 24:16: "The godly may trip seven times, but they will get up again."

Three actions to take

1. Identify what gives you compassion satisfaction.

2. Identify what causes you to have compassion fatigue. What steps can you take to reduce or manage this?

3. What are three ways you can increase self-compassion?

Additional resources and information

Tables one and two on Compassion Fatigue and Compassion Satisfaction – Risk Factors and Protective Factors. See Appendix 1.

For the Professional Quality of Life Scale (PROQOL) where you can download a pdf of the Compassion Satisfaction and Compassion Fatigue (PROQOL) Version 5, 2009, a self-test to identify levels of compassion satisfaction and compassion fatigue, go to https://proqol.org/proqol-measure.

Grise-Owens, Miller and Eaves (2016) *The A-Z Self Care Handbook for Social Workers and other Helping Professionals*, Harrisburg, Pennsylvania; The New Social Worker Press.

Neff, K (2011) *Self-Compassion: The proven power of being kind to yourself*, New York, Harper Collins Publishers.

Amanda M Nickson, Margaret-Anne Carter and Abraham P. Francis (2020) *Supervision and Professional Development in Social Work Practice*, New Delhi, India; Sage.

Chapter 3

The Roadmap to Build Resilience

If you don't make time for your wellness, you will be forced to make time for your illness. We can plan self-care and wellness to build resilience just as we prioritise other important things in our lives.

Building resilience enables us to last the distance. It is good for our mental, physical, emotional and spiritual health. Obstacles become opportunities to shine. Resilience is a skill we can learn and practice, just like any other skill. Dealing with stress and not ending up with chronic stress levels makes a big difference. It is not possible to continually give out to others if your own tank is empty – it is vital to be able to refill your own tank.

To quote a song by Chumbawamba: "I get knocked down, but I get up again. You're never going to keep me down" (1992). This is a good description of resilience – getting up again even when we are knocked down. Without resilience you will get knocked down and are not be able to get back up. Proverbs 24:16 says: "The godly may trip seven times, but they will get up again. But one disaster is enough to overthrow the wicked." (New Living Translation)

What is resilience? A traditional definition would be the ability to bounce back from adversity, but I prefer the definition to bounce forward, to not only come back after setbacks but be further ahead as we have grown and learned through whatever the challenge was. It is not going back to where you were before – it is going forward and making progress.

Self-care is the ability to refill and look after oneself in healthy ways. Some other terms used in this chapter are:

- Stress, which is when an event exceeds a person's resources and endangers wellbeing; and
- Self-care or wellness plans which involve the steps you will take to nurture your emotional, spiritual and physical wellbeing,
- Emergency plan, which means having a self-care plan to use immediately in an emergency situation when we are feeling very stressed.

Self-care plans and ways to build resilience

Having a self-care plan and following through with it – actually doing it – is a way to help build resilience. Self-care puts the responsibility for our wellness on ourselves. There is only so much that can be done if you are overwhelmed with your workload and other factors outside of your control, but there are certainly things in your control that you can work on. Having a written plan

The Roadmap to Build Resilience

that includes a timeframe and a measure for you to hold yourself accountable to achieving a specific goal is very helpful. I have adapted a plan from Grise-Owens, Miller and Eaves who recommend a plan covers multiple areas, including physical care, psychological care, social care, professional, or academic care and spiritual care. I've found using a written plan has worked incredibly well and made a difference in my life.

An example in the physical care area for me is a goal of walking 10,000 steps per day. The accountability measures I put in place included having a Fitbit or a similar tracking device that counts my steps. I also committed to meeting my friend for a walk two mornings a week. On those days, I was much more likely to reach that goal of 10,000 steps than on other days when I didn't have that level of accountability and commitment outside of my own plans.

For my physical wellbeing, I added the goal of getting sufficient sleep each night. I am the type of person who would often be up until 11:00 pm or midnight and still be up by 6:00 am in the morning. I decided that having seven to eight hours sleep each night would be a good goal. To do this, I have needed to go to bed earlier by a conscious decision to do so. It doesn't happen every night, but I have certainly improved and am more conscious of my sleeping habits and the impact of insufficient sleep on my wellbeing.

There are a lot of stressors in our lives that are out of our control, but we can certainly control what we eat and drink and make decisions to eat a healthy diet. Again, having an accountability partner to keep tabs on each other can encourage us in this area.

For spiritual care, I planned to spend half an hour each morning reading my Bible and praying before I faced the day. I have made this commitment a priority. It requires setting my alarm earlier to get up half an hour earlier. You may have a spiritual goal of reading a certain number of books or attending a prayer meeting where you are meeting other people, which can keep you accountable for this goal.

To help manage my emotional wellbeing, I have a plan to help manage anxiety by deliberately planning strategies and goals to overcome this. These have included physical activity, such as walking several times a week and connecting spiritually and emotionally with a close friend who I could share concerns with and know that I wouldn't be judged or thought less of.

While studying towards my PhD, I experienced a period where I felt particularly low and had been diagnosed with depression and anxiety. I had submitted my PhD which was then marked by two examiners. One examiner thought it was of a very good standard and had very positive comments and suggested very few corrections to be made. However, the second examiner thought several chapters needed to be rewritten as they were not up to standard. This examiner wanted another area added to my thesis as well. This feedback and criticism totally knocked me down and I really struggled to get back up. It was only through the support of a few close friends and my family who believed in me and kept saying, "You can do it. You're almost there," that I got back up and was able to complete this huge assignment. I was very close to quitting, even though I had poured in ten years of work and my life into this study and qualification. I did finally submit the reworked chapters and passed my PhD six months later.

Part of resilience is knowing when we want to get back up and not being afraid to ask for the support of people we trust. Rhonda Emonson, a social work colleague of mine, shares her experience of being encouraged:

"While I was undertaking some study in Townsville, Australia, Amanda provided mentoring and a watchful eye. As I was several thousand kilometres away from family and having an innate ability to get just the right balance, she checked in on me regularly, knowing what it is like to be resilient, to have and to execute strategies to last what at the time seemed like a journey that would never end.

"Only towards the end of my time in Townsville did Amanda share her personal and inspiring experiences of how she managed to complete her PhD although experiencing dyslexia and anxiety. Amanda also shared how she suffered a life-threatening accident partway through her studies and it is a miracle she survived and went on to complete her PhD."

What ifs

Objection 1: Isn't self-care the same as self-indulgence?
Response: No. Self-care is vital to our long-term health and wellbeing. Having a self-care plan is an important protective tool, similar to wearing a seatbelt. We put on a seatbelt every day to prevent injuries and death in a serious accident. In the same way, we should view our self-care plan as a tool to automatically put on and implement daily for our long-term protection and care.

Objection 2: I don't have time for self-care.
Response: This is wrong thinking! We need to make time for self-care. This is a priority, or we can end up very ill. Higher stress levels lead to higher risk of heart attack, stroke and many other debilitating chronic health conditions. Self-care is important. Making time for some self-care is vital to build resilience.

A resilient tree - standing strong

Objection 3: I can't do all of this.
Response: Yes, you can. Learning any new skill takes practice and time and practice makes perfect.

The Roadmap to Build Resilience

Start with developing an emergency self-care plan. So, what is your emergency self-care plan? It's thinking of the three things that you know can help you – your go-to actions that help you to de-stress. What are the things that you know help you to de-stress? If you are really, really stressed, they could include:

- Going outside for a 10-minute walk to clear your head.
- Calling your best friend for a chat.
- Listening to a favourite song or podcast and having your earphones ready to go in the top drawer of your desk.
- It could be as simple as doing a deep breathing exercise that you know helps you to calm down.
- You might be a person who loves Sudoku or crosswords and getting immersed in those activities for a few minutes can change your way of thinking. Have a crossword book at the ready in your top draw of the desk or in your bag.
- You might find some mindfulness exercises can work, such as considering What can I see? What can I hear? What can I smell?
- You could also write your emergency self-care plan on a business card or on a sticky note on your computer or desk so that when you are really frazzled, you can pull it out and remember these tips and tricks.

The emergency plan is like a stop-gap measure that can get you through a tough day. If you are needing to use this a few times, this could indicate that you need to do more to reduce stress in your life.

Three actions to take

1. Start planning for resilience by thinking about what you could include in an emergency self-care plan. What are your top three de-stressing strategies? If you don't know, try a few different activities and see what works for you. You may also want to develop a more detailed plan where you work on physical, psychological, spiritual, emotional and professional care.

2. What area do you need to develop in the most to build your resilience? Physical, mental, emotional, social or spiritual? Consider some goals in the area that you think needs most development.

3. What are four new self-care ideas you can try in the next month? There's nothing like trying something new, and if it doesn't work out, you can experiment and can try something else. Find what works best for you.

Additional information and resources

Romans 8:28: "And we know that in all things God works for the good of those who love Him, who have been called according to his purpose."

James 1:2–5: "Consider it pure joy, my brothers and sisters, whenever you face trials of many kinds, [3] because you know that the testing of your faith produces perseverance. [4] Let perseverance finish its work so that you may be mature and complete, not lacking anything. [5] If any of you lacks wisdom, you should ask God, who gives generously to all without finding fault, and it will be given to you."

The Roadmap to Build Resilience

2 Corinthians 1:5–7: "For just as we share abundantly in the sufferings of Christ, so also our comfort abounds through Christ. [6] If we are distressed, it is for your comfort and salvation; if we are comforted, it is for your comfort, which produces in you patient endurance of the same sufferings we suffer. [7] And our hope for you is firm, because we know that just as you share in our sufferings, so also you share in our comfort."

www.theresilienceproject.com

Sam Cawthorn, (2013) *Bounce forward – How to transform crisis into success*, Wiley.

See www.samcawthorn.com

Hugh Van Cuylenburg, (2019) *The Resilience Project – Finding Happiness through gratitude, empathy and mindfulness*, Penguin Random House Australia.

Grise-Owens, Miller and Eaves (2016) *The A-Z Self Care Handbook for Social Workers and other Helping Professionals*, Harrisburg, Pennsylvania; The New Social Worker Press.

Chapter 4

The Power of Professional Supervision

Professional supervision is a game-changer. It provides a safe, confidential space to reflect on what has been happening in your work and it is where you can receive the support to continue. The benefits of professional supervision include:

- Having an opportunity to reflect on the work that you are doing
- Being able to debrief from situations with a trusted, safe person
- Being able to discuss work in a confidential and safe space
- Being able to brainstorm ideas and ways forward and to gain skills and knowledge and helpful feedback to grow

Cox and Steiner (2013) have identified numerous studies that found a correlation between burnout and inadequate supervision for social workers. Similar studies done by Lonne (2003) found a correlation between retention of social work staff who received adequate supervision and professional development and poor retention of social work staff without these. Many people are working without professional support and accountability.

Professional pastoral supervision includes support, self-care, best practice skills, professional development, theological reflection and transformational learning. In social work, Davys and Beddoe describe this concept as "a process of review, reflection, critique and replenishment for professional practitioners" (Davys and Beddoe (2010)). Supervision has elements of education, support and administration. It's a place for learning and a safe space where ethical dilemmas can be discussed. The Chaplaincy Australia website has more information – see the "Additional information and resources" section at the end of the chapter.

Gailene Kaurila, a Scripture Union Chaplain at Ingham State High School stated that: "Professional supervision is the kind of support that a chaplain needs when they are completely immersed in a situation or dynamic and cannot see the forest for the trees. Professional supervisors are the impartial party that doesn't have a stake in the game and can help a chaplain see things from a non-biased position, having no agenda. This is the kind of crucial feedback that every professional needs to remain objective and effective in their work role." Gailene's comments raise the point that supervision can provide objective feedback from someone who is not involved in a situation and help to find the way forward.

Barbara Wheeler-Scott, a Scripture Union Chaplain in Yea, Northern Victoria and the Project Manager for the Centre for Spirituality, Ecology and Wellbeing in Glenburn, has provided feedback on the importance of supervision based on her experiences. The value of social work "grounds" recipients/clients when they access professional supervision. Supervision sessions essentially help you to see your blind spots and act accountably both to yourself and your work. My supervision sessions helped to orient me in especially uncomfortable situations where I was uncertain about who I was. For example, managing one's usual work with the added unpredictability of the pandemic. Supervision with Amanda helped me steer through challenges and to stay focused and on top of situations. This included, for example, in my Chaplaincy role, helping to share the load with the school principal.

To illustrate the second way in which supervision can make a difference, I will share my experience of living in rural and remote Western Queensland. For a few years, I lived in Emerald and covered a huge geographic area across Queensland. I found it very difficult to get adequate supervision in my social work role. Even when I moved to the coast to a larger regional town, it was still difficult to access professional supervision. A group of senior social workers were expected to do peer group supervision, but there seemed to be no structure in place and no one knew what to do. Our time for peer group supervision turned into workgroup meetings simply talking about such things as how to cover staff absences, not professional supervision.

This led to me developing an interest in finding ways to do peer supervision that were productive and helpful for all the workers involved. I ended up doing a PhD in this area of research. The topic I researched was, "Exploring peer group supervision in rural and remote Australia in virtual teams." The importance of connection with like-minded people was very apparent from this study, as well as the need for structure in the discussions. Similarly, being understood by peers of the same profession made a huge difference for several participants in the study and lessened their feelings of isolation.

Another example in my life has been when I recently decided to have a mentor. This helped me to work out some goals and priorities that I'd been grappling with and already has helped me with accountability and timelines. A mentor is an experienced and trusted advisor and "to mentor" is "to advise, support and train". Chaplaincy Australia defines mentorship as "support, encouragement, spiritual reflection, professional mastery and to reflect on ministry and gain a broader perspective. It also provides accountability and areas for growth." Whilst there are some areas that overlap between being mentored and having professional supervision, there are also areas that are distinct to each. Professional supervision is very much focused on the person in the workplace – the impact of work and work situations on the person and how to do the best you can in your role for the people you serve. Mentoring can be much broader and requires you to consider personal goals.

Supervision and mentoring using Zoom

What ifs

Objection 1: I don't have time for professional supervision.
Response: That's exactly when you need supervision to help reflect, prioritise and use your time wisely.

Objection 2: How can I trust an outsider, an external supervisor?
Response: External supervision is helpful because someone outside your organisation provides an objective viewpoint. Your external supervisor is there for you and has no other agenda, so they will be there for your wellbeing.

Objection 3: Professional supervision sounds expensive. I can't afford it.
Response: Your professional longevity and development is worth investing in. Your wellbeing is priceless. Think of professional supervision as an investment into your long-term wellbeing and effectiveness in your role, not as a cost to you.

Objection 4: I don't know any supervisors. Where can I find one?
Response: The Australian Christian Church's website has a section called Chaplaincy Australia that lists several accredited and registered supervisors and mentors. See: www.chaplaincyaustralia.com/supervision

School chaplains employed by Scripture Union Australia are expected to engage a supervisor at least once per school term and can access a list of supervisors on their website. It is part of their professional development.

Other denominations have different supervision arrangements – see their websites for more information. More denominations are requiring regular supervision for their ministers and pastors as part of their professional development.

Social workers are required by their professional association, the Australian Association of Social Workers (AASW), to have regular supervision to remain accredited members of the association. It is a requirement throughout one's career, even for very experienced professionals. Details of where to find a social work supervisor on the AASW website are in the Additional information and resources section at the end of the chapter.

Similarly, numerous other human services professionals have regular supervision for similar reasons. When looking for a supervisor, consider it as you would looking for a good doctor. If you don't feel comfortable or that it's a good match, try a second person until you find someone that you feel comfortable with.

Three actions to take

1. If you do not yet have regular supervision, make a decision to seek this out by the end of this month. Check out who is available in your denomination or workplace. See the resources at the end of this chapter to help you find a suitable supervisor.

2. Think about what you want or expect from supervision. Be ready to share this with your supervisor.

3. Keep notes from supervision sessions. This keeps you accountable if you are going to follow up on something and it helps you to see your progress over time.

Additional information and resources

www.chaplaincyaustralia.com/supervision

www.mentoringnetwork.org which is the Australian Christian mentoring network,

www.aasw.asn.au Find a supervisor https://www.aasw.asn.au/find-a-social-worker/search/

Cox and Steiner (2013) *Self-Care in Social Work, A guide for practitioners, supervisors and administrators*; Washington DC, NASW Press.

Davys, A., & Beddoe, L. (2010). *Best Practice in Professional Supervision*. London: Jessica Kingsley Publishers.

Lonne, B. (2003). Social workers and human service practitioners *Occupational stress in the service professions* (pp. 281–309). Boca Raton, FL: CRC Press.

Nickson, A.M ; Carter, M and Francis , A .P (2020) *Supervision and Professional Development in Social Work Practice*, New Delhi, India; Sage.

Chapter 5

Physical Sustainability

How we look after our bodies makes a difference to our future health and wellbeing.

Having a healthy body helps with our long-term health and wellbeing, both physical and psychological. It is helpful to have energy and physical ability through all stages in life. Physical exercise helps reduce stress levels and strengthens us physically, by supporting our bones and heart. Prevention is better than cure. Good health helps prevent disease and I consider the importance of being a role model for others.

The Bible reminds us in 1 Corinthians 6:19–20: "Don't you realise that your body is the temple of the Holy Spirit, who lives in you and was given to you by God? You do not belong to yourself, for God bought you with a high price. So you must honor God with your body."

Part of honouring my body is looking after my physical health. The Australian Institute of Health and Welfare stated in regards to obesity that in 2017 to 2018, an estimated two in three Australian adults aged 18 years or over were either overweight or obese. Of these groups, they estimated that 36 per cent were overweight and 31 per cent were obese. They have identified that this is a major public health issue, simply because several chronic health conditions and risks increase when we are significantly overweight or obese. The main reason for obesity is explained as being because of a sustained energy imbalance. Many Australians now have a greater energy intake compared to their energy expenditure. Obesity is almost at epidemic proportions. We need to be proactive if we do not want to be part of these health statistics. Physical activity can help use up the energy (food and drink) we consume to help us maintain a healthy weight and improve our fitness. Exercise releases endorphins in the brain, which help us to feel good.

Physical spaces, such as being out in nature, are also good for our mental health and physical health. I know personally that sunrises, feeling a breeze and breathing fresh air is very good for me and I really enjoy it – once I get there. I can battle getting up earlier to make the time to get to that walk and beautiful part of the world to see the sunrise, but once I do, the rewards are great.

What is physical sustainability all about? Fitness is the condition of being physically fit and healthy. Some consider health as being free of illness or injury and a person's mental or physical condition. Health is defined as "a state of complete physical, mental and social wellbeing and not merely the absence of disease or infirmity" (World Health Organisation, 1946). The Oxford dictionary defines wellbeing as the state of being or doing well in life and being happy, healthy or prosperous in condition. Sustainability is the ability to be sustained, supported, upheld or confirmed. Another word for sustainability is resilience, stamina

Physical Sustainability

or achievability. If we are going to be sustainable, physically, we need to be working on our wellbeing, our fitness and our health.

So, how can I do that? I have never been a very sporty person, but I do greatly enjoy bushwalking. I thought, well, if I need to be healthier and fitter because I want to be on this earth for as long as I can, I need to plan and do something myself to stay physically active. One of the ways I have found helpful to do this is that I connected with a couple of friends who were also wanting to get fit, and we were also wanting to lose some weight. We planned to do some walks together. Because I had to meet a friend at a certain time at a certain place, it meant that I went for those walks in the morning. If it had been just me deciding to go, I would probably have simply rolled over in bed when the alarm went off and thought, "No, I'll go tomorrow."

Another way to make a commitment to going on a walk and holding yourself accountable to that is walking for a cause. I've walked in the Mito Foundation's The Bloody Long Walk three times to fundraise for this charity. The commitment to walk in a fundraising event on a certain date has meant I have signed on the dotted line and showed up on the day. I have found sponsors to support me and so I trained to walk a much further distance than I would normally walk. The Bloody Long Walk is often done by people training to do marathons as the event is 35 kilometres. I have managed to walk 23 kilometres each of the three times I have done this fundraiser.

Mito Foundation,
The Bloody Long Walk Sydney, 2019

Physical Sustainability

Blue Dragon Children's Foundation Walk,
Townsville, 2021

I have also walked shorter walks for other charities, such as for the Blue Dragon Children's Foundation in Vietnam. That, again, is a win-win: I'm supporting a worthwhile cause, the charity is receiving donations and I am sufficiently motivated to follow through on the exercise involved. I have swum laps for ReachOut, a mental health service reaching young people in particular; I have done push-ups to support veterans at risk of suicide; I have walked kilometres to fundraise for people living with multiple sclerosis and for those affected by dementia and for several other charities. For more details regarding charity walks you could join, see the "Additional information and resources" section at the end of this chapter. It has been very satisfying being motivated and doing those walks. The benefit I've noticed is that I have had more energy and I feel more positive after completing the walk, which leaves me more able to do new things.

A few years ago, I decided to do a very large walk called the Camino Way in Spain. This was part of a long-awaited and planned overseas holiday – my trip of a lifetime. A close girlfriend and I were in training for several months beforehand as we were both unfit and had no idea how we were going to do this long walk. Over time, with consistent effort, we were able to get fitter and do that walk in Spain. It was also a reward because it was an amazing overseas holiday and experience, which allowed me to have time alone with God in the beautiful rural Spanish countryside. I was being refreshed and rejuvenated. You may not be able to go overseas as that is not an everyday type of holiday and certainly travel opportunities have changed with COVID, but I believe that you can certainly create your own break away from your usual routine and be refreshed. I like to create what I call "Camino experiences" where we plan, even if it's a day away or a weekend away, somewhere in nature, where you can be refreshed and renewed in spirit. I will often accompany that experience with a walk.

Another way to improve your health and wellbeing to make sure that you have enough sleep. This may sound like getting back to basics, even boring or common sense, but it is the basics that keep us healthy. If you are constantly burning the candle at both ends – getting up early, but also staying up very late at night, is it any wonder that you are very fatigued and at risk of burnout? You need to know your own body and how much sleep you need to function well. If you know, for example, that you function best on eight hours of sleep, are you getting that much sleep each night?

There is a lot of literature now on ways to help people sleep better. If some people find it difficult to get to sleep, having done some physical activity during the day can really help that process. And it is recommended not to have screen time immediately before going to bed. So, whether that is watching television, a computer screen, mobile phone screen or any other screen, the blue light affects your ability to turn off and go to sleep because it stimulates our eyes and sets off our body clock thinking it's daytime. I have found if I read a novel that will often help put me to sleep just before I go to bed. Looking at paper rather than an electronic device can make a difference.

Another strategy is to look at our diet. Whilst this topic may not be popular, I have noticed the difference between when I'm eating healthier food and when I am eating junk. I'm not saying never have a treat and never have junk, but maybe it's time to revisit and examine what you are eating? What am I putting in my body? Is that food going to fuel me well to do the things that I need to do. If you find that you already have some concerns about what to eat or are already overweight or even obese, it would be wise to see a dietician, someone who can advise the best way for you to lose weight. That's a challenge for me as well. I'll never get back to the body I had in my twenties, but I want to be fit and healthy and able to function the best I can for as long as I can. I want to be able to do whatever I'm doing well so that I can serve with excellence and not be serving out of breath because I am so unfit. There is a whole industry built around sports and exercise science with university-qualified people that can help with programs to help people such as you and me with our health. Why not access some of these fantastic resources that are specifically catered to the needs of the Australian population?

In the "Additional information and resources" section at the end of this chapter you will find information about dietitians, sports exercise physiologists and other professionals who can help you with your goals around fitness and health. Some people decide to join a gym, where you will have access to personal trainers who can create a fitness program specifically designed for your needs.

Since COVID has taken over our world, there have been jokes about having a "COVID belly" or the "COVID diet" and how people have been putting on weight because of being stuck in their homes in lockdown. Many of us are in sedentary jobs, sitting at computers, on Zoom meetings and on the phone. Any way that you can increase your activity, including at home, is beneficial. I have started a practice of walking around if I'm on a phone call rather than being continually sedentary. If you are in a role where you are in lots of Zoom meetings, maybe investigate having a sit-stand desk set up so that you can alternate between sitting and standing.

I'm sure a couple of generations ago, people couldn't imagine how sedentary our life would become. Many of us drive vehicles or sit in trains to get to workplaces. Fewer and fewer people would be in the position to walk to work or bicycle to work. Many of us now work in a home office, due to COVID restrictions or because the world has changed since COVID and more and more people are working from home. Consequently, we need to schedule and add exercise into our lives because it does not usually occur in our daily routines.

What ifs

Objection 1: I don't have time.
Response: Make the time. Your health is irreplaceable. If you become seriously unwell, that is going to have a major impact on your life. I would much rather put in the effort now in prevention than being in the position of having to recover from a major ill health event.

Objection 2: I don't know what to do.
Response: You can try a physical activity that you have done in the past and enjoyed or try something new. Either way, just do

something! You could see a sports exercise physiologist who can assess your current level of fitness and help you work on whatever areas you want to work on.

Objection 3: I don't have the motivation.
Response: If you struggle with the motivation or feel that you are not the "sporty type", arrange to meet someone and do an activity together. That keeps you accountable and, in my experience, makes it happen.

Three actions to take

1. Plan a physical activity to do this week. Commit to meet a friend for a walk or a run or at the gym. Choose something that you would enjoy or would like to try.

2. Ask yourself, "Am I getting enough sleep?" If you're not sure how much sleep you are having each night, record it for a week. There are sleep apps that can help you with this if you don't know. If you aren't getting enough sleep, choose to go to bed earlier and review your routine before bed. If you're having trouble getting to sleep, do you need to cut down the screen time you have in the evening? Make a change.

3. Review your diet and even your caffeine intake. If you are lacking energy or possibly overweight, consider, are there healthier foods you could add into your diet this week? Could you reduce the number of less healthy meals that you have?

Additional information and resources

https://www.healthline.com/

https://www.aihw.gov.au/

https://www.aihw.gov.au/reports-data/behaviours-risk-factors/overweight-obesity/about

To find a dietician go to: https://dietitiansaustralia.org.au/ then there is a tab, Find a dietician.

To find an exercise sports scientist or physiologist visit https://www.essa.org.au/, then the tab Search for an accredited sports scientist.

World Health Organisation. (1946, June). *Constitution of the World Health Organisation.*

https://www.who.int/about/governance/constitution

For more information on some of the causes mentioned in this chapter and others I have walked or swam for, see these websites

https://secure.fundraising.cancer.org.au/

https://www.mito.org.au/

https://www.bluedragon.org/

https://forums.au.reachout.com/

https://www.dementia.org.au/

https://www.themay50k.org/

Apps:
Neuro cycle app: How to be mentally healthy – help set habits and goes for 63 days.

Other apps are also available to help with relaxation exercises.

Sleep app is another app.

Chapter 6

Emotional Sustainability

Emotions affect how we think, feel and respond. Having good emotional health and emotional intelligence are keys to emotional resilience. The benefits of having emotional sustainability include being emotionally healthy which is good for our overall wellbeing and health.

Knowing and understanding our emotions helps us to have control over our emotional responses. Emotional intelligence equips us as leaders to be able to understand the emotional responses of others. Having emotional sustainability and control helps us to be a good role model for others.

God created us as emotional beings. It is part of being human and we are created in God's likeness. Jesus himself showed many different emotions. For example, the Bible records that He was angry, He wept and that He showed compassion. In John 11:35 it says: "Jesus wept." This was when He came to see Lazarus who had died. Mary greeted him at the door and was very sad. Matthew 9:36 says: "When he saw the crowds, he had compassion on them because they were harassed and helpless, like sheep without a shepherd." To deny our emotions is not healthy or helpful to our own health. Managing emotions is a skill which can be learned.

So, what is emotional health? It is all about how we think, feel and behave. It is our sense of wellbeing and ability to cope with life events. Being emotionally healthy means you are aware of your emotions, whether positive or negative, and that you can deal with them effectively. It does not mean that you are happy all the time. Emotionally healthy people still feel stress, anger and sadness, but know how to manage their feelings well.

Emotional intelligence is the ability to manage both your emotions and to understand the emotions of the people around you. This is essential in leadership positions. Emotional intelligence (EQ) contains several facets. Most writers in the literature talk about self-awareness, self-regulation, motivation, empathy and social skills. More information on emotional intelligence is in the "Additional information and resources" section at the end of this chapter.

How do we manage emotions and create emotional sustainability in our lives?

Firstly, we need to recognise our own emotional state. If we are upset or angry, it is important to look at why rather than just pretending it's not there. If we can find out what the cause and the source of our emotional response is, then we can do something about it.

Emotional Sustainability

This may mean accessing professional help. If you are going through a particularly difficult time, such as a life-threatening health diagnosis for yourself or a loved one, a grief reaction, or extreme frustration because of things in the workplace that are out of your control – whatever your reaction, if you find that this is taking over your thinking more than you would like it to, that might be an opportunity to seek some professional help. Professional help could include accessing professional supervision or seeing a counsellor, social worker, psychologist or mentor.

I once experienced a period in my life when I was feeling extremely stressed, overwhelmed and frustrated in my workplace. I went to see a psychologist who was able to give me perspective on the things that I can change and control and she reminded me that there are some things that I cannot. If there's someone safe that you can talk to about things that are affecting you and your emotions, that can be helpful and make a difference. Some workplaces have Employee Assistance Programs (EAP) that their employees can access, where the employer pays for the counselling sessions for the employee.

Secondly, being able to identify and calm emotional people around us is a great skill to have as a leader. This is achieved through emotional intelligence and good social skills. There was a time when I was working for a government department as a senior social worker, when a very distressed woman came into the office and several other staff were rolling their eyes. This was a woman who had done the rounds of several other agencies, going over and over her story – talking in circles. She spoke so quickly that it was hard to get a word in edgeways.

Her circumstances were complex. Homelessness was part of the story, as were mental health issues. I was asked to speak with this woman. I sat with her and listened to her story. When she had finished, I said to her, "You sound very frustrated and upset." She stopped and said, "You are the first person who has heard what I've been saying." It is interesting that because I identified and named the emotions that she seemed to be feeling and experiencing, she felt heard. Other people had repeated back to her the content of her situation, her homelessness and other circumstances, but no one else had identified and spoken out loud the emotions that she was feeling. It was a moment of breakthrough for her, as well as for me and the agency I was working for. When you are with people who are experiencing any number of emotions – anger, sadness, frustration – often naming that emotion or checking it out is a way to connect with that person. I have often tried saying, "Have I heard this correctly? You sound very upset," or, "You sound very angry and sad." I find this is a great way to connect with that person. If you get the emotion wrong, don't worry, as people will correct you.

This knowledge of identifying the correct emotion and being able to name it can be empowering for people who may not be as skilled in understanding emotions themselves and why they are behaving the way they are behaving.

A third way I have found for managing difficult circumstances is by noticing what is positive in my life and being thankful for it. One way to do this is to keep a gratitude journal. I have kept a gratitude journal during a very difficult period of my life, when one of my children was encountering serious mental health problems. I could have let this circumstance smother me, and I was already carrying guilt around her having mental health issues. I determined I needed to focus on what good there was in my life and how God had been faithful to me. I decided to keep a journal of three things I was grateful for every day for a year. This started as an easy enough process. I was thankful for a roof over my head, that I had an income and that I could meet my needs for food, shelter and transport as I had a car that I could afford to buy petrol for. After a few weeks, it became harder to think of three things that I was grateful for every day.

I could think of how God had answered my prayers in the past and come through for me. I was thankful for the beauty of His creation – for such things as a beautiful blue sky, for colourful butterflies in my garden. I could think of so many things that I was thankful for. Over time, as the months went by, my worry, anxiety and emotional state about my daughter's ill health receded into the background because I could see how faithful God had been, time after time. The gratitude diary changed my thinking because I knew I didn't have to worry – God had everything in his hands.

Keeping a gratitude diary, particularly if you are going through a challenging time, is an excellent strategy to support your emotional wellbeing and emotional sustainability.

What ifs?

Objection 1: Surely emotions are not that important?
Response: Yes, they are. They affect our thinking, feelings, actions and behaviour. They are the source of nearly everything we do.

Objection 2: This self-awareness sounds very self-centred.
Response: Being aware of your own emotional responses means that you can respond well to others.

Objection 3: What if I can't manage my emotions like anger?
Response: We can all learn and take little steps, one step at a time. If you are having significant issues, see a counsellor such as a social worker or psychologist for help. They have expertise in working in these areas.

More information on how to find a social worker or psychologist are at the end of this chapter under "Additional information and resources".

Three actions to take

1. Become more aware of your emotions and emotional responses. Keep a journal of these for two weeks

2. Read and learn about emotional intelligence. See the "Additional information and resources" section below.

3. Notice the emotional responses in others around you. Can you identify the emotions?

Additional information and resources

To find a social worker or psychologist. You can look on their professional association websites. See the links, www.aasw.asn.au/findasocialworker

Or www.psychology.org.au then the tab, find a psychologist

Or https://ccaa.net.au/ to find a Christian Counsellor.

Further information is available at www.beyondblue.org.au

Dr Caroline Leaf has several books, including *Helping our mental health and emotional wellbeing* and *Cleaning up your mental mess* and her website www.drleaf.com has some other podcasts, apps and resources.

The neuro cycle app, *How to be mentally healthy, help set habits* goes for 63 days. It's well worthwhile.

Emotional Sustainability

Workshops and professional development sessions can be tailored to specific requirements on emotional resilience, intelligence and sustainability by Dr Amanda Nickson – see at the end of book for more details or visit www.amandanickson.com.au

For training in emotional intelligence, life and leadership development, see Facebook: VIGEO Life and leadership development https://www.facebook.com/vigeoleadership/ with Camillus De Almeida.

Chapter 7

Psychological Sustainability

How do we sustain a healthy mind and stay fresh?

When we are psychologically healthy, we are able to stay mentally fresh and be open to new ideas. This stops us stagnating where we are and increases a sense of wellbeing.

If we are psychologically healthy, we can confirm and know that we are in a good place. Ready to take on new and challenging knowledge is so accessible today with technology – there is so much at our fingertips, such as YouTube and podcasts. There are an infinite number of resources ready to be accessed.

Psychological health can also depend on whether you have encountered some of the more serious and worrying aspects of life. Sadly, in some workplaces, bullying, intimidation and vicarious trauma can occur and a serious traumatic event could lead to post traumatic stress disorder (PTSD). These can all occur in leadership roles and workplaces, whether in a paid position or as a volunteer, and can adversely affect our mental health. In this case, you need to access professional help and support. Sometimes, you can feel stuck or trapped in a certain role or job because you may be the main breadwinner, or need the income and are worried that if you chose to leave a job, would you get another job? Sometimes leaving a workplace or moving roles can be a smart move to be well long-term.

Ongoing stress from bullying and intimidation can lead to depression and anxiety, and even to suicide. Don't be fooled thinking that this could never happen in the organisation you are working for, whether that is a church, a Christian organisation or any human service organisation. It happens, probably a lot more than you realise.

So, what does the term psychological mean? Dictionary Online defines psychological as affecting or arising in the mind, related to the mental and emotional state of a person.

In this chapter, I also refer to academic wellbeing, which relates to education and scholarship to educational learning. One way to be psychologically refreshed might be to an attend a conference or an inspiring meeting with like-minded people. I recently attended a state conference of the Australian Christian Churches and I found it reignited my passion and purpose. I was excited and challenged by many of the sessions and heartened as pastoral professional supervision was being promoted by the State Executive members and the benefits of professional supervision were being explained. The State Executive members had tried professional supervision, often for the first time. Sometimes they were sceptical, but they all came back with stories of how much benefit it had been to them and now recommended it to other pastors and leaders.

Psychological Sustainability

Another segment of the conference was dedicated to discussing community engagement. This is another passion of mine as I believe that the church should be serving in the community, meeting needs and being relevant to the people around them. This was very encouraging to me as these two areas are important to me and give me much of my purpose. Attending that conference was another way to sustain me.

I realised I needed help for my psychological wellbeing at a time when I was in a stressful work environment, which resulted in me reaching out to a counsellor for support. The workload seemed overwhelming, and accessing a psychologist gave me some strategies for dealing with the situation that I could not have otherwise come up with myself. The benefit of seeing a psychologist in this situation was that she was external to my workplace, totally objective, had no agenda and was able to advise and support me.

Another way in which I can be refreshed is listening to podcasts in the car. Podcasts can change my mindset by challenging, refreshing and inspiring me with new ideas. I can listen while travelling, so they are always accessible. I know some pastors and leaders who listen to podcasts while walking or exercising, filling their minds with new and exciting thoughts. At the end of this chapter in the "Additional information and resources" section is a list of some sources of podcasts that might be helpful for you in this area. Attending networking meetings in a district or a region where again, you can meet with people who might be in similar roles and positions can be helpful.

Another way to help our psychological sustainability is to be clear on roles and expectations. If you are in a volunteer role in a leadership capacity, sometimes there can be expectations from so many different people, both above and below you, that can be difficult to negotiate.

If there is a clear role statement and expectation in writing, that can be helpful. There are numerous additional pressures on pastors in church life that can take their toll.

A few thoughts about the challenges in ministry come from Pastor Geoff Hollands, a former ACC pastor: "It's lonely at the top. Living in a goldfish bowl takes its toll on both oneself and one's family." He found that insecurity amongst leaders and pastors was fairly common and rather self-perpetuating. Pastor Hollands went on to say that there was a pressure to perform both from people in the congregation and those above you, which added to pressure. The inability to be transparent with your peers for fear of criticism could be crippling. Every leader needs a non-judgemental friend or a friend who can honestly and unconditionally speak into your life.

What ifs

Objection 1: There are so many other things to do. Isn't this just more pressure? I don't have time.
Response: Looking after our psychological health is beneficial and the way we refresh will be different for everyone, but it is absolutely worthwhile and important. Having time is always about priorities. You can make time if it is important to you. Everyone gets 24 hours a day.

Objection 2: Taking time out for professional development, such as going to a conference, can be expensive. I can't afford it.
Response: Consider it an investment. It is very important to invest into your knowledge and the networking opportunities of a conference. It could be well worth your while.

Objection 3: What if I feel trapped and too scared to say anything about the bullying, intimidation or trauma I'm experiencing?
Response: This is exactly when you need to see either a professional supervisor or a social worker or a psychologist because they will be able to support you and help you with a way forward. The longer someone stays in a situation where they are bullied or intimidated is what can contribute to significant mental health challenges including depression, anxiety and even suicidal thoughts. Vicarious trauma is another area where it is better to talk with a professional sooner rather than later. The longer you take to address concerns and not deal with issues, the longer it takes to recover and the harder that road is. Don't put off what you can do today. Keeping one's head in the sand is not a solution.

Having hope is important. Isaiah 40:29–31 says: "He gives strength to the weary and increases the power of the weak. Even youths grow tired and weary and young men stumble and fall; but those who hope in the Lord will renew their strength. They will soar on wings like eagles; they will run and not grow weary, they will walk and not be faint."

Three actions to take

1. Find an inspiring speaker online that you like to listen to, such as through a podcast, and set aside some time, even half an hour, during the week to listen, or you could read about a topic that you are interested in

2. Review if there are any areas of serious concern in your current situation, such as bullying, intimidation, depression and anxiety. Book an appointment this week to see a professional supervisor, social worker or psychologist. Don't put it off.

3. Consider if there is any other study or learning you would like to do. Find out about it then decide if you want to enrol in that course or listen to that podcast. This helps you to stay fresh.

Additional information and resources

For podcasts there are many available under Joyce Meyer podcasts:

https://podcasts.apple.com/au/podcast/joyce-meyer-enjoying-everyday-life-tv-audio-podcast/id152564324

https://joycemeyer.org/

https://elevationchurch.org/podcast/ Steven Furtick podcasts

https://podcasts.apple.com/us/podcast/elevation-with-steven-furtick/id216015753

https://drleaf.com/pages/podcasts Dr Caroline Leaf podcasts

Psychological Sustainability

For supervision, look at https://www.chaplaincyaustralia.com/supervision-2 where you can scroll through a number of supervisors and find one that might suit you.

To find a social worker: https://www.aasw.asn.au/find-a-social-worker/search/

To find a psychologist: https://psychology.org.au/about-us/contact-us/aps-find-a-psych

https://emmaus.org.au/ – gatherings, retreats, prayer walks – renewing Christian disciples

https://www.blackdoginstitute.org.au/

Chapter 8

Social Sustainability

Why be social? God created us as social beings. It is not good for us to be alone. The benefit of being social is that it builds connection and community. It can help us overcome feeling isolated and alone. Being social offers companionship and support and often involves hospitality and being neighbourly. It contributes to feelings of wellbeing and being part of a collective.

Mental and physical health can be improved through greater social connection and strong relationships, as isolation negatively affects our mental health and wellbeing. Those with the poorest social relationships have more than double the risk of depression compared to those with high quality connections (www.healthline.com). Recent increases in poor mental health due to social isolation have been highlighted in the media during the many COVID lockdowns and restrictions experienced by countless people in recent months. The mental health organisation Beyond Blue states that three million Australians are living with anxiety or depression. Social isolation can cause a range of adverse health effects ranging from sleeplessness to reduced immune function. Loneliness can result in higher anxiety, depression and suicide rates.

As an adjective, being social means needing companionship. The opposite is being lonely, which is defined as being sad because one has no friends or company. Being in community is how God created us to be, not living in isolation.

Isolation, the process or fact of isolating oneself or being isolated, is something that many more people are now aware of since the COVID pandemic. For many people, being unable to connect physically with family members, loved ones, friends and usual social groups has had a marked effect on their mental health and wellbeing. For those living in aged care facilities in Australia, the frequent lockdowns and limits on social interaction, whilst potentially assisting with physical health, have had untold negative impacts on the mental health of many individuals. Countless individuals have experienced "forced" isolation because of health directives and have experienced the negative mental health impacts because they lived more than five kilometres away from friends and loved ones.

Isolation can be a coping strategy chosen for short term relief when feeling overwhelmed. An example from my own life is that I'm aware of my own behaviour and patterns. If I am very stressed and close to burnout, I find myself isolating myself from friends, becoming a hermit. I call it feeling "peopled-out". This could be from being invited to a social event that usually I would enjoy attending and want to go to, but I find myself declining or making excuses not to attend. This strategy of isolating oneself may give some relief short term, but it didn't help me long-term. In fact, I felt like I was warring against myself. I was craving social connection and support, but I was too exhausted to make the social engagement and connections I needed which could have provided me with support and improved

Social Sustainability

my general wellbeing. I finally connected with a close friend who would meet with me, pray with me and that made a big difference. Connecting socially one-on-one seemed more manageable and a connection with another person who I perceived as "safe" and supportive was invaluable.

A second way of increasing social connection for me has been connecting with people outside of my church or work and creating new friendships. I joined a book club and met a new group of people who have become friends. This group have been a great source of laughter and encouragement and connection. I have recently joined a gym where I meet many new people and have the opportunity to connect socially for a coffee after a group exercise class. This level of connection is the beginning of forming new relationships. It is important to make opportunities in our week for a balance between work and play or between work and family time.

A third way in which I have been able to increase social connection and really enjoy life is having celebrations with social events. I will often plan a birthday party or an anniversary event and celebrate milestones by inviting friends. People really enjoy being able to get together socially and just relax with good food and a good laugh. Celebrating a Midwinter "Christmas in July" or finding another excuse for a gathering is important in building relationships. I enjoy hosting events that serve as fundraisers for different charities, community organisations or needs in the community, such as an afternoon tea or other gathering for people to enjoy fellowship and fun. If you are worried about an event or feeling like you're not a hostess or host material, you can always arrange to meet at a coffee shop or meet at a park and have a picnic or a barbecue where everyone brings their own food. Choose your favourite place, giving opportunity for people to get out of their homes and connect with others. This does wonders for the soul. Proverbs 17:22 says: "A

Afternoon tea celebrating life

cheerful heart is good medicine, but a crushed spirit dries up the bones." I find meeting with others can cheer me up – it does us good.

Another way of strengthening my social sustainability has been to seek out and reconnect with friends with whom I have lost contact over time. I had a close friend at university, Mary Anne, who I lost touch with when she and her husband moved overseas. Years later, I was able to track her down on Facebook. When I reached out and reconnected, we were both so excited and able to pick up our friendship from years before, as if there had not been any missing years in between. We now connect much more regularly. When I visited Sydney, where I was born and raised, I was able to see her in person which was fantastic. Mary Anne was very grateful that I sought her out, and my life is richer from knowing her and reconnecting with her and her husband and her family.

A high tea celebrating friendship and life

As it says in Hebrews 10:24–25: "And let us consider how we may spur one another on toward love and good deeds, not giving up meeting together, as some are in the habit of doing, but encouraging one another—and all the more as you see the Day approaching."

What ifs?

Objection 1: What if maintaining relationships takes time and effort?
Response: Yes, it does, but the time and effort are absolutely worthwhile. Strong relationships and staying in communication with friends and loved ones can support good mental health.

Objection 2: Making time for social activities is a luxury. I am not able to fit that in my week.
Response: You may think that, but having social connection is good for you and it is good for your mental health. Making the time to catch up with one friend for a coffee or for a walk may in fact help you be in a better headspace to do all that you need to do that week. Social connection can re-energise you.

Objection 3. I've lost contact with so many of my friends and family over time. I have no one to connect with that I am close to.
Response: Reach out to them. I have found people are absolutely thrilled when I have made the effort to reconnect with friends, some who I have not seen for years and we have been able to rebuild our relationship.

Three actions to take

1. Ring a friend and reconnect with them this this week.

2. Arrange to meet a friend at least weekly, whether that's for a walk, a meal or a coffee. This person could be outside your work group or church group.

3. Meet some new people and make new friends. Invite someone over. I know for introverts, it can be scary making new friends, putting yourself out there and inviting people, but it is absolutely worth the effort. The rewards of friendship are great, and warrant stepping outside your comfort zone to connect with someone. You may be meeting a need in that person for connection as well.

Additional resources and information

More information on the effects of social isolation and loneliness is available at: https://publichealth.tulane.edu/blog/effects-of-social-isolation-on-mental-health/

For more psychological support, www.beyondblue.org.au has numerous resources and contacts regarding support if you are feeling particularly socially isolated with depression or have social anxiety or suicidal thoughts.

Chapter 9

Spiritual Sustainability

Sustaining the spiritual part of ourselves is the most important. Our spirit lives forever and is our true self. There are many benefits in a resilient spirit. Spiritual growth and strength sustain us and can sustain a strong faith that does not waiver in the storms of life. Leaders shine when we have a personal experience with God. We need to have fresh spiritual food, like "manna" (that God provided to the Israelites daily when they were in the desert, according to Exodus 16:31) on a daily basis, not stale spiritual food or old revelations from previous years. Our true self is our spirit. Our body is a vessel for the spirit. Many people are actually spiritually starving. They have no spiritual food, or very little, and then wonder why they are hungry, thirsty and dry. We make time to have physical food and drink daily – usually several times a day – but are we feeding ourselves the spiritual food we need to sustain our spirit?

Psalm 23 states: "The Lord is my shepherd. I lack nothing. He makes me lie down in green pastures. He leads me beside quiet waters. He refreshes my soul. He guides me along the right paths for his name's sake. Even though I walk through the darkest valley, I will fear no evil for you are with me; your rod and your staff, they comfort me. You prepare a table for me in the presence of my enemies. You anoint my head with oil, my cup overflows. Surely goodness and love will follow me all the days of my life. And I will dwell in the house of the Lord forever." Verse 3 of this Psalm particularly speaks to me where it says, "He refreshes my soul." This is true spiritual sustainability that can be provided by God and God alone.

Spiritual sustainability means having spiritual wellness and spiritual good health.

Spiritual wellness can be described as being spiritually healthy. We feel more connected to God and to others. We have clarity with choices and our actions are more consistent with our beliefs and values. Spiritual health is achieved when you feel at peace with life and when you are able to find hope and comfort, even in challenging circumstances. Taking care of our spiritual health or having spiritual care is important.

Spiritual care is any support related to questions about life's meaning, depending on your values and beliefs, which is included in many health care and palliative care provisions, encouraged by state health departments as it is seen to have value and importance. See the "Additional information and resources" section at the end of this chapter for a link to this information.

There may be times in the wilderness where there is struggle, where we may have felt abandoned by God with a prayer not being answered the way we hoped or when we have felt spiritually barren or dry. So, how do we not only bounce back but bounce forward from such times? How can we replenish ourselves spiritually?

Spiritual Sustainability

An example from my own life of how I've tried to build my spiritual sustainability has been by turning on praise and worship music or singing and worshipping God whilst playing the piano. Listening to songs of praise and worship, even when I don't feel like it, can refresh my spirit and bring me closer to God. In fact, choosing to praise, particularly when I don't feel happy with my circumstances, is a sacrifice that can change the atmosphere to one of hope and faith and build our spirit and our faith.

Another way to build our spiritual sustainability is spending time alone with God and reading his Word, the Bible and seeking and asking God for understanding of what we are reading. God's Word (The Bible) is a Living Word – *rhema* – so reading the Bible is not just like reading a book. God's words in the Bible come alive and God can speak to us about his plans and purposes for our lives through His Word if we allow the time for Him to do that.

Being refreshed in God's presence is another way of building my spirit, through praying, talking to God, but also listening to Him, waiting for Him to speak into my heart. Matthew 11:28–29 says: "Come to me, all you who are weary and burdened and I will give you rest. Take my yoke upon you and learn from me, for I am gentle and humble in heart, and you will find rest for your souls." Spending time with God by praying shouldn't be a one-way conversation, but a two-way interaction. There have been times when my prayers have seemed like a list of my concerns that I am wanting help from God with; but I am reminded that Jesus has taught us how to pray in Matthew 6:9–13. It says: "This then is how you should pray. Our father in heaven, hallowed be your name, your kingdom come, your will be done, on earth as it is in heaven. Give us today our daily bread and forgive us our debts. As we also have forgiven our debtors. And lead us, not into temptation, but deliver us from the evil one." This gives us a blueprint of how we are to pray – first praising and acknowledging and thanking God for who he is.

Our Father in heaven, praying to do his will on earth as it is in heaven, praying for provision, praying for forgiveness for our sins by confessing them and that we forgive others. Forgiving others is often a key to letting go of things that can otherwise cause us bitterness. This prayer is a template of how to pray and is a great key to spiritual sustainability. When we have spiritual knock-backs, like a prayer not answered or the answer is not the one we were hoping for, this can add to our character and our story. Rom 5:3–5 (NLT) reminds us that: "We can rejoice, too, when we run into problems and trials, for we know that they help us develop endurance. And endurance develops strength of character, and character strengthens our confident hope of salvation. And this hope will not lead to disappointment. For we know how dearly God loves us, because he has given us the Holy Spirit to fill our hearts with his love."

What ifs

Objection 1: Aren't our physical and mental health much more important than our spiritual health?
Response: They are important, but equally, or probably more so, is our spiritual health.

Objection 2: It doesn't really matter, does it?
Response: Yes, it does! Our spirit is the main part of us. It's who we are on the inside. Our spirit lives forever.

Objection 3: It's hard to hear from God. I don't know how to do it.
Response: Well, press in – spend more time in God's presence, in reading his word, in seeking Him and you will find Him. Keep

Spiritual Sustainability

Time with God (Bible, journal, pen and a cuppa)

going. You can speak to other believers about how to do this and read more about this.

Three actions to take

1. Spend some time this week praising and worshipping God by singing or listening to praise and worship songs. Decide to commit to doing this regularly.

2. Find a place where you can seek God and read the Bible each day. This may be in a favorite chair in your house or in a quiet park or part of the garden. Expect to hear from God. Spend time talking with God, but also allow time to hear from Him. Decide to make time each day to read some of the Bible. It is our guidebook for life, but more than that, it's God's Living Word to us. We need this spiritual food daily, just like we need physical water and food to nourish us.

3. Choose to fellowship or meet with other believers. This can build your faith as we can encourage each other. It can start with deciding to contact someone, to meet with someone, or to attend a connect group, attend a church service so that you can grow in faith from hearing the testimony of God's work in other people's lives and of answered prayers. You will be reminded that God is alive and active and cares about the lives of people.

Additional information and resources

https://www.biblesociety.org.au provides daily readings that you can subscribe to.

https://www.biblegateway.com provides access to numerous translations of the Bible and has a search function to help you find the verses or topics that you are wanting.

https://www.youversion.com/the-bible-app You version has a free app that can be downloaded on your phone that can send you a verse of the day every day and has many different reading plans on different topics that you can search for by topic.

Vision Christian radio station, a national radio station, has a website, www.vision.org.au and an App so that you can play recent stories, interviews, music, testimonies – all things that encourage your faith.

Listen to a local Christian radio stations and be encouraged. Many also have websites with further resources, podcasts and apps.

Many different Christian pastors and speakers can also encourage and build our faith and build our spiritual sustainability. For example, you can find podcasts or online resources from Joyce Meyer, Stephen Furtick and many others.

https://www.betterhealth.vic.gov.au/health/servicesandsupport/Palliative-care-emotional-spiritual-and-cultural-care

Chapter 10

Empowering Emerging Leaders

Encouraging resilience in emerging leaders is critical for the future of Christian leadership in Australia. The benefits include being able to last for the long-term and making leadership sustainable. Learning good habits and boundaries early can save emerging leaders from burnout down the track. Any new skill can be learned, so start now. Ministry can be both fulfilling and exhausting, so it's important to get the balance right.

I have seen many ministers who do not take holidays each year, or even a few days off, and therefore model being workaholics, setting this example for their leadership team and emerging leaders. This is concerning. Wayne Crockford, a university chaplain for 17 years, offers some comments on the risks and pressures for Christian leaders that can contribute to stress, burnout or compassion fatigue. He stated: "Performance – I must be busy to prove my worth" and, "The demands of the church board and congregation to perform in ways that are not my gift. I am not saying everything has to be from the gift – all are required to "muck in" together to see something done. Keep this sensible, simple and practical, down to earth and realistic." The pressures of expectations from leadership above you and the expectations of those you serve can contribute to you never stopping and therefore never being able to feel refreshed.

What does the Bible say about this? 1 Peter 5:2–3 (NLT) offers advice for elders: "Care for the flock that God has entrusted to you. Watch over it willingly, not grudgingly – not for what you will get out of it, but because you are eager to serve God. Don't lord it over the people assigned to your care but lead them by your own good example." Then in Titus 1:7–9 (NLT) says: "A church leader is a manager of God's household. So, he must live a blameless life. He must not be arrogant or quick tempered. He must not be a heavy drinker, violent or dishonest with money. Rather, he must enjoy having guests in his home and he must love what is good. He must live wisely and be just, he must live a devout and disciplined life. He must have a strong belief in the trustworthy message he was taught. Then he will be able to encourage others with wholesome teaching and show those who oppose it, where they are wrong." Then Titus 2:6–7 (NLT) says: "In the same way, encourage the young men to live the wisely. And yourself must be an example to them by doing good works of every kind. Let everything you do reflect the integrity and seriousness of your teaching."

So, what is a leader? A leader is the person who leads or commands a group, organisation or country. A dictionary defines "emerging" as "becoming apparent or prominent". Other words that are used to define leadership include influential, charismatic, visionary, servant, inspirational, humility, sacrificial, motivator, rebel, trustworthy, determination, passion and creativity (www.hellosplice.com)

Empowering Emerging Leaders

In my role as a professional pastoral supervisor, I have spoken with numerous chaplains and leaders who are doing amazing things, often involved in many different community activities in the area that they live, some working full- or part-time and doing church or chaplaincy roles on top of this. Many are also doing studies that are required for their chaplaincy or leadership role and are juggling their family and life around a huge workload and responsibilities, whether in paid capacities or voluntary. I have found, I often need to give them permission to say no to some requests and set boundaries. I have needed to remind and encourage them that it is alright to take time off for a holiday, to have a sick day when they need it or to take a day off as a carer because they have sick children. Many of these emerging leaders struggle with expectations. They are so willing to please and serve that they're not looking after themselves or their families. I have had feedback from some chaplains after these sorts of discussions that they are so relieved that they have now been able to have that time off or felt confident to negotiate, whatever it is that they were fearful to do.

One way you can help emerging leaders is to have realistic, not unrealistic, expectations of them. If someone has a clearly defined role, even a written role description or duty statement, that gives them some parameters of what is expected. Encouraging a work-life balance in church life or in the role as a chaplain or leader is a good way to form positive habits early. It is important to have the balance between work and time off, otherwise family life, including marriages breaking down, can be the casualty. I recently had a discussion with Pastor Peter Aspin, a former ACC pastor, who was talking about leadership. He stated that leading is serving for a season, laying a foundation and preparing to pass the baton on to someone else. Change and transition are the norm in church life, setting it up for the next phase. He loves to encourage and mentor young leaders and to see them succeed and do well.

Informal mentoring is important. The Bible gives us some examples of emerging leaders: Timothy, Titus and Barnabas all served under a great leader, Paul, and their stories in the Bible offer insight into their mentorship.

Sometimes we can be aware that the balance is wrong but we are unsure how to change it. We all have 24 hours a day which gives us 168 hours every week. Do an audit of your week by keeping track of how many hours a week you spend doing different activities. How many hours do you spend working, sleeping or serving as a volunteer as a chaplain or at church? It all adds up. What about family time, such as eating meals together or spending time with your children? Study, exercise, recreation, travel? The following two pie charts give examples of, firstly, an unbalanced life and, secondly, a more balanced life. Consider your own situation. Are there adjustments that you could make to lead a more balanced week and life?

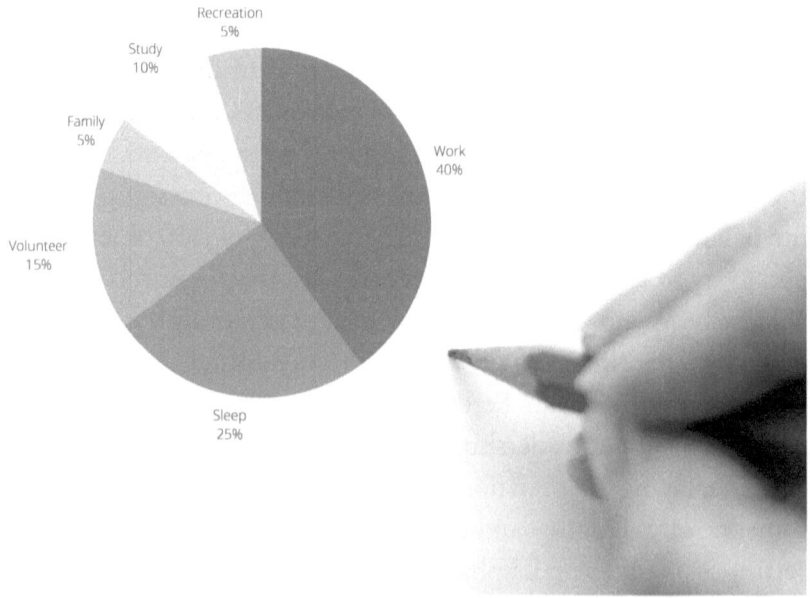

An unbalanced life

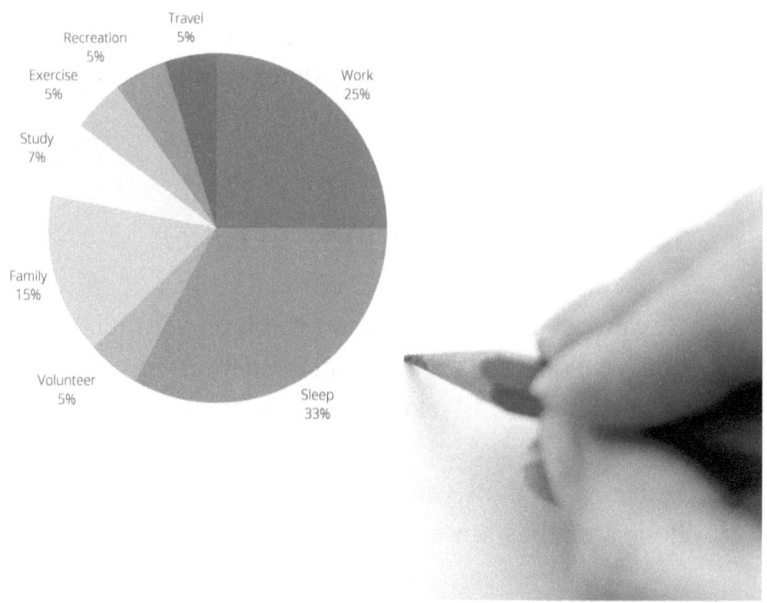

A more balanced life

What ifs

Objection 1: I have often heard the statement "emerging leaders need to toughen up."
Response: No, they need to learn balance in life from the start of their journey if they want to go the distance and be sustainable.

Objection 2: Emerging leaders are young and energetic. They should be able to do everything.
Response: No, they should have choices, not unrealistic expectations imposed on them by others.

Objection 3: I have heard some senior leaders say that "I had to do everything at their age."
Response: Just because you may have done something in the past doesn't mean it is the best way.

There is an interesting debate about whether leaders are born or made. Jay Reynolds discussed this and quotes recent scientific studies that suggests leadership is 30 per cent genetic and 70 per cent learned.

Three actions to take

1. Review whether you have too much on your plate. Do you have time for self-care and to do the things you love to refresh yourself? Do you have balance?

2. Is there an activity you have felt compelled or obliged to do that really you wanted to say no to? Be assertive.

3. If you are a senior pastor or leader, encourage your leadership team to seek balance in their lives. This includes taking regular time off for holidays. Encourage emerging leaders to have regular professional pastoral supervision. Are you leading by example and role modelling balance, taking leave and having regular professional supervision? Do you have a self-care plan covering the different areas of sustainability (emotional, physical, psychological, social and spiritual) that you can share with your emerging leaders and encourage them to develop a plan of their own?

Additional information and resources

J Reynolds, (2021) Born leaders versus made leaders, https://www.unboxedtechnology.com/blog/difference-between-born-leader-and-made-leader/

Creating a pie chart of how you spend your time can be an eye-opener. You can create pie charts in Canva – see https://www.canva.com/

Or see the link:

https://joshmartinink.wordpress.com/2010/06/15/how-to-make-a-work-life-balance-pie-chart/

More on work-life balance – "The Life Career Rainbow: Finding a work-life balance that suits you":

https://www.mindtools.com/pages/article/newCDV_95.htm

Chapter 11

The Encouragement Ethos

A word of encouragement can make all the difference between keeping going or giving up. The benefits of encouragement are that when we encourage others, we are taking part in God's nature. When our actions encourage others, we are acting like Jesus. True encouragement gives God's hope and courage to others. The giver feels blessed too. You know how good it feels to be encouraged.

1 Thessalonians 5:11 (NLT) says: "Therefore, encourage one another and build each other up, just as you are already doing." Hebrews 3:13 says: "But encourage one another daily." Hebrews 10:24–25 (NLT) says: "Let us think of ways to motivate one another to acts of love and good works; and let us not neglect our meeting together as some people do but encourage one another. Especially now that the day of his return is drawing near." Hebrews 12:1 (NLT) states: "Let us run with endurance the race God has set before us." It is so much easier to continue on that path with the encouragement of others.

The Dictionary Online definition of "to encourage" is "to give support, confidence and hope to someone." It is the giving of courage and help. Encouragement is the act of encouraging or a state of being encouraged.

Some examples from my own life where encouragement has made a huge difference include the time when I was struggling to finish my PhD. I was full of self-doubt. I mean, I was really struggling – paralysed by fear. A few close friends kept telling me, "You can do it." They believed in me and encouraged me to keep going, whereas left to my own devices, it would have been so easy to give up. I finally did complete my PhD and am very grateful for all the encouragement and prayers of friends along the way. Being with someone going through a hard time can make such a difference, even if we are unable to change the situation.

How often do we take the time to notice people and thank them for what they are doing well and give positive feedback? I have seen young leaders being pulled up for something they have not done well or for something that has been missed. Yes, we need to improve, but how often do these leaders get encouragement that they have done so many other things well? It is easy to take people for granted. Recognising a job well done, or someone's faithfulness in doing even small things for others or at an event, is critical to keeping these leaders on for the long term.

I used to find it very hard to receive positive feedback and I would either deflect any compliment or thanks or outright challenge it by saying it wasn't right. I have since learned the value of accepting credit when it is due, so now I absorb it. It took some emotional work to feel comfortable with doing this. Accepting positive feedback gracefully sets an example for a team to share more praise and positive feedback with each other. We want to be in the

The Encouragement Ethos

business of building each other up, not tearing each other down, which is so much of what happens in some workplaces. It is easy to underestimate the impact of a simple phone call or a text message that might encourage someone when they are on your heart.

I remember hearing a story of a young boy – I'll call him Jake – who was struggling carrying a whole pile of schoolbooks walking home from school one day. He seemed to have every book he owned in his arms and in his backpack. Another boy, Pete, who lived nearby, noticed him and offered to help and started chatting with Jake. Pete didn't know Jake very well. Jake was fairly new at school, and Pete started to become friends with him while walking home that day. Years later, Pete heard from Jake that the day he had been walking home from school with all those books, he had decided to end his life. Jake was clearing out his desk so that he didn't leave that job at school for someone else to do. The interaction with Pete on that day, simply having someone who was friendly and encouraged him and talked about spending time with him the next day, was enough to turn Jake around. He now had hope for the future.

We don't know what people are going through. We may know just a small part of someone's story or situation. Just actively listening to someone and offering encouragement can make such a difference. In my role as a professional supervisor, I see myself sometimes as a "professional encourager". People will pour out what they're doing in their lives. I notice what a good job some of them are doing and give that feedback. Often these pastors or chaplains don't get much feedback at all, except when they've missed something. I think it is so valuable that positive feedback and praise is given when it's due.

Thankyou card and teapot

What ifs

Objection 1: I just don't know what to say.
Response: I suggest being honest and thank people for what they are doing for how it impacts you. Thank them for their efforts, for their faithfulness. Notice and acknowledge effort and good work.

Objection 2: It won't make any difference.
Response: You don't know that. Giving some positive feedback might be the word of hope that encourages someone to keep going and to not give up. It may encourage someone to keep making a difference.

Objection 3: I don't want to give someone a "swollen head".
Response: You won't. Everyone needs encouragement. It helps with motivation, confidence and gives the message that they are valued.

One way of showing encouragement is through acts of kindness. As I stated in my book, *Living by Faith: How the impossible becomes possible with God* (2020), "A small act of kindness can be the difference that helps someone who might be at the point of breakdown and turn it into a breakthrough."

Three actions to take

1. Identify two leaders who you can encourage this week. Think of how you will do this. You may decide to send a text, ring them up, or meet for a coffee.

2. Think of people who have encouraged or nurtured you in your faith and leadership over time. Thank them for this. Acknowledge them. This could be by sending a thank you card, a letter or an email. Do it!

3. Can you think of other people you know who could do with some encouragement? Make the effort and phone them or contact them – notice and encourage them.

How can we encourage ourselves? The Bible has many verses that can encourage us in our faith. Some of these are noted in the "Additional information and resources" section below.

Additional information and resources

https://faithhacking.ca/5-things-to-do-when-you-need-encouragement-5042d76d5c23

www.indeed.com/career-advice/career-development/positive-feedback-examples

https://faithhacking.ca/

Books:

Amanda Nickson (2020) *Living by Faith: How the impossible becomes possible with God*, Diamond Creek, Victoria; Ultimate World Publishing.

Bible verses that can encourage:

Galatians 6:2; Romans 8:31; John 14:27; Psalm 31:24; Romans 15:2; Philippians 1:6; Psalm 121:1–2; John 16:33, 1 Corinthians 10:13; 1 Corinthians 16:13; Romans 15:5; Proverbs 18 :10; 2 Cor 1:5; Romans 1:11–12; Psalm 90:17; 2 Corinthians 1:5; 2 Corinthians 4:16; Isaiah 40:31; 1Timothy 4:12; Joshua 1:9; 1 Corinthians 15:58, 2 Timothy 1:7.

Chapter 12

Walk the Path for Others to Follow

As a leader, how can you influence policies and practices to safeguard future and emerging leaders? There are many benefits in ensuring the wellbeing of emerging and future leaders – ensuring that leaders can last long-term in ministry and service. This could mean making changes so that emerging and future leaders are supported better in what they do. It also provides the opportunity to develop and leave a positive legacy. It is important to encourage changes so that the mistakes of the past are not repeated by leaders in the future.

This draws me to look at policy and practices. What is a policy? The Dictionary Online defines a policy as "a course or principle of action adopted or proposed by an organisation or individual". Similar to a blueprint, a policy is a strategy, plan or approach. Practices are the application or use of an idea, belief or method as opposed to the theories relating to it.

How can we influence policies and practices to improve the sustainability of emerging and future leaders? I try to walk the talk since my own experience of burnout and compassion fatigue a few years ago. I have put into practice a self-care plan and given it a much higher priority in my life. I have incorporated goals, plans and added in accountability across the five areas that I consider essential. I block out times in my diary and treat these activities like appointments. These include activities that support my emotional, physical, psychological, social and spiritual sustainability, all to build my resilience as a leader. It is working!

In the last few months, I have found a mentor who I am happy to work with and I am having regular mentoring sessions. I continue to have regular professional supervision sessions. I am doing everything in my power to keep my wellbeing and health on track.

Finding and reviewing existing policies in your organisation could be useful. If there is no policy that covers anything along the lines of self-care, supervision, having mentors or having regular leave, maybe consider how to influence the development of a policy on sustainable leadership or work-life balance. Who could you engage to help with this task? Is there a policy document in a similar organisation you could look at? Even starting to have conversations in the workplace about this, by raising awareness, can make a difference.

If you are a leader in a team, can you share ideas on self-care with your team in the team meeting? Can you check in on how everyone is going and show that you care? Can you offer to have a social worker or psychologist come in to facilitate a training session on the importance of stress management and self-care planning? It's important to have conversations with our teams. Have you explained what professional supervision is and encouraged pastors and leaders to have regular supervision? Many denominations are now introducing the need for regular professional supervision for their ministers, pastors and leaders. Chaplaincy Australia provides supervisors for pastors, chaplains and leaders. Scripture Union Australia requires school chaplains to have regular supervision as part of their professional development and good practice principles. Let's embrace this recognition of the need for support in a role that many have done unsupported for a long time.

What ifs

Objection 1: I had to become a leader with little support so the new ones need to toughen up. There was nothing wrong with the "old ways".
Response: Just because you survived the isolation and stress of leadership when you were an emerging leader doesn't mean that you do not take the opportunity to make the path into leadership better and more sustainable for the emerging and future leaders who follow.

Objection 2: There are other priorities to put resources into.
Response: Yes, there are always many other priorities, but I am suggesting that there is no greater resource than your people and your leaders. It is worthwhile investing in the sustainability of current and emerging leaders.

Objection 3: I have not managed to get a self-care plan that is working for me yet.
Response: You have a great opportunity to be transparent and suggest to your team that you can all work on this together – yourself included – in developing self-care plans and ways to make them a priority in your lives.

Three actions to take

1. Look at current policies or your employment contract and see where improvements could be made to support leaders in their role. Put a policy review or a duty statement review on the agenda for the next board or committee meeting or schedule a meeting with the senior leader.

2. Consider who you could talk to or influence about making positive changes to the volunteer policy or training manual in your organisation.

3. Review or reflect on whether your church, non-governmental organisation or employer considers its staff and/or volunteer welfare seriously. If it doesn't, consider how could you start this conversation and with who?

Additional information and resources

Books:

Wayne Cordeiro *Leading on empty: refilling your tank and renewing your passion* (2010).

Carey Nieuwhof *Didn't see it coming: overcoming the 7 greatest challenges that no one expects and everyone experiences* (2018) Waterbrook, USA.

Peter Scazzero *The Emotionally Healthy Leader* (2015).

Peter Scazzero *Emotionally Healthy Spirituality: It's Impossible to Be Spiritually Mature, While Remaining Emotionally Immature* (2017).

There are also other books by Peter Scazzero on similar topics.

Sean Nemecek https://pastorsoul.com/ for articles, books, coaching.

Walk the Path for Others to Follow

Podcasts

Carey Nieuwhof and YouTube channel – see www.careynieuwhof.com podcasts.

Sean Nemecek **https://pastorsoul.com/podcast/** Hope Renewed Podcasts.

Appendices

Appendix 1

Nickson, Carter and Francis' Compassion Fatigue Protective and Risk Factors, Table 11.1 on page 204, **Nickson, Carter and Francis (2020) Supervision and professional development in SW Practice**

Protective factors	Risk factors
Undertaking personal therapy	Emotional exhaustion
Ongoing supervision	Physical exhaustion
Sense of meaning in their work	Spiritual exhaustion
Safe and respectful workspace	Impaired judgement
	Excessive caseloads
	Toxic workspaces
Continuing education	Professional isolation
Social connectedness	Little or no supervision
Professional connectedness	Professional disappointment
	Professional isolation
Reasonable case load	Loss of energy
Peer support	Insomnia

Protective factors	Risk factors
Profession self-care plan	Loss of purpose and meaning
Balanced and nutritious diet	Reduced self-esteem
Regular physical exercise	Concentration difficulties
Sufficient sleep	Decision making difficulties
	Preoccupation with the client's suffering
	Dealing unsuccessfully with boundaries
	Countertransference
	Burnout
	Little or no professional self-care
	Minimal ongoing professional education

Appendices

Appendix 2

Nickson, Carter and Francis' Compassion Satisfaction Protective and Risk Factors, Table 11.2 on pages 205 – 206, **Nickson, Carter and Francis (2020) Supervision and professional development in Social Work Practice**

Protective factors	Risk factors
Balanced and nutritious diet	Emotional exhaustion
Regular physical exercise	Physical exhaustion
Sufficient sleep	Spiritual exhaustion
Doing one's work effectively	Loss of energy
Enjoyment of work	Loss of purpose and meaning
Emotionally positive, supportive and respectful workspaces	Concentration difficulties
Reasonable workloads	Preoccupation with the client's suffering
Monitoring workloads	Dealing unsuccessfully with boundaries
Establishing and maintaining boundaries	Countertransference
Debriefing with colleagues	Excessive caseloads
Self-awareness	Burnout
Sound ethical reasoning	Little or no supervision
Regular supervision	Little or no professional self-care
Peer support	Minimal ongoing professional education
Maintaining work-life balance through practices such as self-compassion, journaling and practicing mindfulness	Toxic workspaces
	Professional isolation
Professional self-care goals integrated into learning contracts	Minimal processes (e.g., intake, session notes, case notes, referral, self-harm)

Protective factors	Risk factors
Develop and implement an individual self-care plan	Limited or no induction
Supportive induction processes	
Transparent processes (e.g., intake; session notes; case notes; referral; self-harm)	
Continuing education	

Permission / Copyright Information Regarding Appendices

Originally published in *Supervision and Professional Development in Social Work Practice* Copyright 2020 © Amanda M. Nickson, Margaret-Anne Carter and Abraham P. Francis. All rights reserved. Reproduced with the permission of the copyright holders and the publishers, SAGE Publications India Pty Ltd, New Delhi.

This permission pertains only to Table 11.1 on page 204 and Table 11.2 on pages 205 – 206. authored by Amanda M. Nickson, Margaret- Anne Carter, Abraham P. Francis from the book – *Supervision and Professional Development in Social Work Practice* (ISBN: 9789353286637)

All quotations from the Bible are from the New International Version unless otherwise indicated.

Afterword

Congratulations on reaching the end of *The Resilient Leader*! Are you ready to put what you have learned into action?

Before you do, I have an important question to ask you: Do you know Jesus Christ as your personal Lord and Saviour? Are you ready now to put things right between yourself and God? Perhaps you used to believe and have a close personal relationship with God, but there has been some time away from God? The Bible teaches us that, "All have sinned and fall short of the glory of God" (Romans 3:23). Sin is simply our separation from God. Romans 6:23 states that: "The wages of sin is death, but the gift of God is eternal life in Christ Jesus our Lord." Jesus has made a way for us to be able to restore our relationship with God.

John 11:25–26 states: "Jesus said to her, 'I am the resurrection and the life. The one who believes in me will live, even though they die; and whoever lives by believing in me will never die. Do you believe this?'"

If you would like to have a new life and a fresh start with Jesus as your Lord and Saviour, it is as simple as having this conversation, just speaking directly with God. You can repeat these words or say something similar:

> *"Thank you, Lord Jesus, that you died for my sins. Forgive me for all I have done wrong and for not having you as the Lord of my life. I accept you now, Jesus, as my Lord and Saviour. Help me to follow you and live for you. Amen."*

Congratulations! You have restored your relationship with God. This is the most important step in our lives – it means you can be assured of eternal life with Him.

To build your faith and resilience, apply some of the principles discussed in this book – spending time getting to know the Bible and reading, studying and learning some of the scripture will help build your spiritual sustainability.

Spending regular time in prayer to have a conversation with God – He wants to have a close relationship with you.

Find people who can encourage you in your faith and you them. This could include finding a local church that you can be part of. Look for a church that is friendly and helps you to grow in faith with good teaching.

Practise gratitude. Try a 30-day gratitude challenge – keep a journal and write down three things you are grateful for each day for 30 days.

Look after yourself and find ways to replenish your tank – physically, emotionally, psychologically, socially and spiritually. This is important!

Show compassion to others.

Ask God to guide you in what your next steps are.

More resources to help you develop resilience on your journey in life are available on the website:

http://www.amandanickson.com.au/

About the Author

Dr Amanda M Nickson is a wife, mother, social worker, Christian pastor, author and speaker.

Amanda grew up in Sydney, with her parents (until their separation when she was 17) and younger sister. Her childhood was spent participating in a range of musical activities, including piano, choirs, chamber music and orchestras. She also loved playing tennis. After finishing school, Amanda studied social work at the University of New South Wales. She became actively involved in her local church youth group, went on beach missions and enjoyed bushwalking. After graduating, Amanda started working as a social worker in Western Sydney before moving to Central Queensland.

Amanda chose social work as her profession as an extension of her Christian faith, to help and serve others in their time of need. She has worked in a variety of positions in government, non-government organisations, academia and private practice, across a range of fields – community development, individual and family work, group work, community education – in which she has covered issues as diverse as child protection, juvenile justice, adoptions, health, defence, homelessness, domestic violence, finance and refugees.

Amanda has also lectured in social work for 13 years at James Cook University in Townsville. She currently runs her own business, Interactive Solutions, www.interactivesolutions.org.au providing training, supervision, social work services and organisational consultancy services.

Amanda returned to study to gain her PhD in social work and is recognised in her field as an expert in social work supervision. Whilst an accomplished professional and public speaker, Amanda focuses her energy in this book on equipping others with the skills and knowledge to become sustainable leaders and build their capacity for resilience.

Amanda has been a Christian for over 40 years and has served as a leader in various positions in her local church. She is a pastor with Australian Christian Churches (ACC). Her Christian faith and beliefs are at the core of everything she does, and she also holds a Diploma of Leadership from Alphacrucis College. In addition, Amanda is a registered supervisor with Chaplaincy Australia and Scripture Union Australia. Her passion is to encourage others to become resilient leaders while enjoying the journey so that they thrive, not just survive.

Amanda lives in Townsville with her husband, one of her three adult children, her dog, Scruffy, and her cat, Kitty. She loves nothing more than catching up with friends over a cup of tea, especially Devonshire or high tea, and making time to walk in nature in the beautiful national parks nearby and further afield.

Other Books by the Author

Amanda Nickson (2020) *Living by Faith: How the impossible becomes possible with God*, Diamond Creek, Victoria; Ultimate World Publishing.

Amanda M Nickson, Margaret-Anne Carter and Abraham P. Francis (2020) *Supervision and Professional Development in Social Work Practice*, New Delhi, India; Sage.

Amanda Nickson (2021) Chapter 15: *Supervision in isolated and rural settings*, in O'Donoghue, K and Engelbrecht, L *The Routledge International Handbook of Social Work Supervision*, Oxon and New York, Routledge.

Acknowledgements

I am thrilled that this book has become a reality and I truly hope it brings you great encouragement.

First, I would like to acknowledge God and thank Him for all He has done in my life and all He has brought me through. With God, I have learned resilience and sustainability.

The gift of faith in Jesus Christ is life-changing. It brings hope. I appreciate and would like to thank and acknowledge the influence and gift of time and encouragement of many Christian pastors, leaders and fellow believers in my life in many different places who have helped me to grow in faith.

I especially want to acknowledge the love and support of my family who have encouraged me in this journey as an author of this book. To my husband, Daryl, and my children, Jessica, Danielle and Timothy – thank you!

For my friends who have been interested in and supportive of my book-writing venture – your words of encouragement have meant the world to me. I would particularly like to acknowledge and thank those men and women of faith who have so generously given of their time to write a testimonial for this book: Penny Mulvey, Susan Marcuccio, Ps Cami de Almeida, Rev Ann Harley, Dr Rhonda Emonson and Jennifer Blackshaw. I have been truly humbled and encouraged by what you have said. Thank you from the bottom of my heart.

To the ministers, chaplains and leaders who have contributed comments and ideas from our conversations for inclusion in this book – thank you for your availability and honesty: Rev Mal York, Ps Peter Aspin, Ps Geoff Hollands, Dr Rhonda Emonson, Chaplain Wayne Crockford, Chaplain Gailene Kaurila and Chaplain Barbara Wheeler-Scott. Thank you for your enthusiasm and for contributing valuable words of wisdom.

To my close friends who keep encouraging me – especially Wendy Stuart Smith, Suzanne Bravery, Louise Ingram and Ps Mark Baker – thank you!

To the amazing photography by Rachael Bourke, of Be Still Bourke Photography, who captured some wonderful photos of me for the front and back cover of this book – thank you.

To Natasa Denman and the publishing and mentoring team at Ultimate 48 Hour Author, thank you so much for your support, wisdom and guidance in the writing and publishing of this book. Your influence has made what seemed out of reach – writing this book – not only possible but also enjoyable along the way. Thank you for investing your time and expertise in me.

Speaker Bio

Dr Amanda Nickson is the author of *The Resilient Leader: How to beat being overwhelmed and burnout for sustainable leadership.*

A highly regarded speaker and teacher in her professional life as a social worker and pastor, Amanda has a PhD in Social Work and is recognised in her field as an expert in social work supervision.

An accomplished professional and engaging public speaker, Amanda is focusing on her passion to equip others, especially leaders, to live life to the full and avoid the traps of exhaustion and burnout.

Experienced as a professional supervisor for Pastors in the Australian Christian Church (ACC), Chaplains with Scripture Union (SU) and human services workers in numerous government departments and non-government organisations, Amanda shares a well-grounded perspective on the way forward for empowering existing and emerging leaders.

Amanda's passion is to help others in sustainable leadership roles and equip leaders with a roadmap to build resilience. With her passion and expertise, she easily connects with her audiences, leaving them motivated and inspired.

Amanda's keynotes, which can be customised to suit any audience, include:

1. How to Win the Burnout Battle
- Understanding compassion fatigue and compassion satisfaction
- How to balance work and life
- Sustainable practices

2. Equipping Leaders for Sustainable Leadership
- The roadmap to build resilience
- Emotional sustainability and emotional intelligence
- When to say no and other strategies

3. Empowering Emerging Leaders
- Knowing your spiritual health and other indicators
- Learning good habits and boundaries early
- Powerful encouragers – mentors and supervisors

To enquire about booking Amanda to speak at your leadership group, church or next event, email:

amanda.nickson4@gmail.com

or phone: 0415989896

Amanda is available to travel to speak in rural and remote areas and welcomes this opportunity.

More details can be found at:

https://www.amandanickson.com.au/

Offers and Call to Action

Offer 1

A free copy of Chapter 1 – available as a sampler as a PDF which is great to share with others who may be interested. Available at http://www.amandanickson.com.au/

Offer 2

Building Resilience – a 12-week course (online). See my website at http://www.amandanickson.com.au/ for details and mention this offer for a 10 per cent discount.

Offer 3

Engage Dr Amanda Nickson as a speaker or trainer for you next event, leaders' meeting or staff retreat.

Amanda's keynotes, which can be customised to suit any audience, include:

1. How to Win the Burnout Battle
- Understanding compassion fatigue and compassion satisfaction
- How to balance work and life
- Sustainable practices

2. Equipping Leaders for Sustainable Leadership
- The roadmap to build resilience
- Emotional sustainability and emotional intelligence
- When to say no and other strategies

3. Empowering Emerging Leaders
- Knowing your spiritual health and other indicators
- Learning good habits and boundaries early
- Powerful encouragers – mentors and supervisors

To enquire about booking Amanda to speak at your next event or for availabilities, email:

amanda@amandanickson.com.au

or amanda.nickson4@gmail.com

Notes

The Resilient Leader

Notes

Notes

Notes

www.ingramcontent.com/pod-product-compliance
Lightning Source LLC
Chambersburg PA
CBHW021153080526
44588CB00008B/316